Also by M. A. Demers

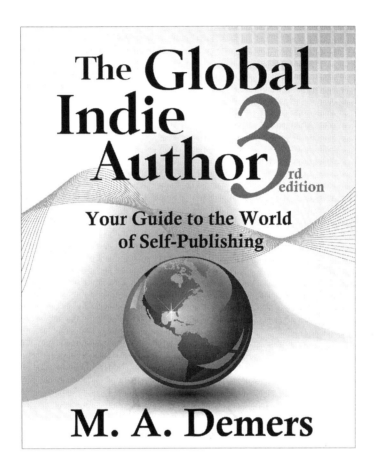

The *Global Indie Author* covers all aspects of self-publishing including:

* Book Structure * Manuscript Editing * Copyright and Registration
* Copyright and Trademark Infringement * Libel, Obscenity, Hate Literature, Civil Liability * The ISBN System * Software
* Print Production * Marketing * Distribution and Royalties
* Payments and Withholding Tax * The Vanity Press Machine

Available in both print and ebook

Fiction by M. A. Demers

Baby Jane

The Point Between: A Metaphysical Mystery

Connect with M. A. Demers on

Her website (www.mademers.com)

Facebook (https://www.facebook.com/M-A-Demers-Writer-and-Fine-Art-Photographer-110443572340945/timeline/)

Twitter (@mademerswriter)

Goodreads (http://www.goodreads.com/author/show/4774449.M_A_Demers)

Wattpad (https://www.wattpad.com/user/MADemerswriter)

Build Your Own eBooks For Free!

A Step-by-Step Guide to Formatting and Converting Your Manuscript into ePub and Kindle Books Using Free Software

M. A. Demers

Published by Egghead Books, Canada

www.mademers.com

Copyright © 2017 Michelle A. Demers
INSI 0000 0003 5669 426X

Published by Egghead Books, 2017

All rights reserved under International and Pan-American Copyright Conventions. No part of this book may be reproduced in any form or by any electronic or mechanical means, including information storage and retrieval systems, without permission in writing from the author, except by reviewer, who may quote brief passages in a review.

Cover design by Michelle A. Demers. Background design based on an image by Gerd Altmann. Many thanks.

Library and Archives Canada Cataloguing in Publication

Demers, M. A., 1964-, author
    Build your own eBooks for free! : a step-by-step guide to formatting and converting your manuscript into ePub and Kindle books using free software / M.A. Demers.

Issued in print and electronic formats.
ISBN 978-0-9916776-7-2 (softcover).--ISBN 978-0-9916776-8-9 (EPUB).--ISBN 978-0-9916776-9-6 (Kindle)

    1. Electronic publishing--Handbooks, manuals, etc. 2. Self-publishing--Handbooks, manuals, etc. 3. Kindle (Electronic book reader). 4. Electronic books. 5. File conversion (Computer science)--Handbooks, manuals, etc. I. Title.

Z286.E43.D446 2017   070.50285'416   C2017-901669-5
    C2017-901670-9

Contents

Is This Book For You?	1
What You Will Need	3
eBook Development	6
Characteristics of eBooks	7
Reflowable eBooks	7
Fixed Layout eBooks	9
PDFs	10
Language Options	10
1 Format Your Manuscript	11
Language Settings	11
Document Properties	13
Document Set-Up	13
The Importance of Using Styles	14
Fonts	20
Cutting and Pasting	24
Blank Lines and Line Breaks	24
Page Breaks	26
Dashes	26
Ellipses	26
Footnotes	27
Internal Hyperlinks	28
Miscellaneous Formatting Principles	28
Save as Web Page, Filtered	30
2 Build Your eBook	32
Step 1: Import Your HTML File Into Sigil	32
Step 2: Delete Font Definitions	35
Step 3: Create Your Stylesheet	35
Step 4: Clean Up Your Stylesheet	38
Step 5: Clean Out Your Document	50
Step 6: Create Your Links (optional)	58
Step 7: Create Your "Page" Breaks	60
Step 8: Add Your Cover	62
Step 9: Build Your Table of Contents	68
Step 10: Add Your Metadata	71
Step 11: Validate Your ePub	73
Step 12: Test Your ePub	75
A Word About Publisher Formatting	78

3 Convert to Kindle	79
Step 1: Delete Cover File	79
Step 2: Specify Cover	79
Step 3: Remove Apple Cover Code	80
Step 4: Edit TOC	80
Step 5: Add the HTML Table of Contents	80
Step 6: Add Start Reference	82
Step 7: Update Metadata	83
Step 8: Convert to Mobi File	83
Step 9: Test Your File	86
4 Advanced Formatting	90
Creating New Style Classes	92
New Character Classes	93
Multiple Classes	94
Controlling Emphasis	95
Adding Color	95
Font Color	97
Lines	97
Blockquotes	100
Text Boxes	101
Tables and Columns	104
Lists	110
Editing the HTML TOC	113
Font Embedding	114
Internal Images	122
Inline Images	131
Frames	131
Kindle Media Queries	134
Endnotes	135

Is This Book For You?

Do you want to:

- Avoid the cost of ebook conversions?
- Have control over the look and function of your ebooks?
- Create professional-quality ebooks you can be proud of?

If so, then this book is for you.

With the free, easy-to-use program Sigil, the savvy self-publisher can build an ePub for upload to retail sites such as Kobo or Apple, then make a few modifications to the ePub and upload it to Kindle Direct Publishing for conversion to Kindle. Or you can convert it yourself using Amazon's free Kindle Previewer.

Other free software can be used to test your files before you upload them to retail sites. If you write your manuscript in an open-source word processor such as OpenOffice, then even that is free.

What I love most about using Sigil is that *I* control the look and feel of my ebooks. Many conversion companies simply use template code they have developed for efficiency and cost-effectiveness but which doesn't leave much room for creativity. If you want anything different you have to pay extra—if such options are offered at all. But with Sigil you can create the ebook *you* want and at no extra cost. It's a win-win.

Even if you choose to hire out the design of your ebook, having Sigil on hand and understanding its basic functions means you can later make file changes without cost. If you find typos in your manuscript and want to fix them, or if you publish another book and want to add advertising matter to your earlier ebooks, you can do this yourself rather than pay a conversion company again. Modifying your files will become *very* expensive if you have to pay someone every time you need to update your ebook. [1]

If you are an author who wishes to sell only on Amazon's Kindle Direct Publishing, you can bypass learning Sigil and instead upload an

HTML document exported from your word processor. However, your manuscript will still need to be properly formatted (Chapter 1), and the HTML document will still need to be modified (Chapter 2). It will still be recommended that you convert with and test your file in Kindle Previewer (Chapter 3). You will find, then, that **not only does uploading an HTML document restrict your options, but you don't save yourself much time or effort over working with Sigil.** And as you work through this manual you will find that taking that extra step into Sigil is not a difficult one.

* * *

When Amazon first launched Kindle Direct Publishing in January 2010, the retail giant and ebook innovator accepted just about any text document for conversion to the Kindle format. Problems quickly arose for users, who discovered that the auto-conversion method wasn't as successful as Amazon claimed: many such ebooks suffered from odd formatting behaviour, or simply looked dreadful. These problems continue to this day, and in fact have increased.

Many authors then try but fail miserably to use auto-conversion tools such as Calibre or Smashwords' Meatgrinder to build ePubs and mobi files. After tearing their hair out to no avail, these authors are often advised to resort to the nuclear method: save their manuscript as text only, then reformat the whole thing again. Needless to say, such a drastic option is enough to make any author of a 300-page manuscript want to cry.

But if you use Sigil, resorting to the nuclear method will never be necessary: you will be able to easily find and delete any problems in your manuscript. The result will be a clean, stable, well-functioning ebook.

Many authors find the idea of working with HTML code to be too daunting. But you do not need to understand the code or how it works; you only need to be able to follow the directions outlined in this manual. It is a bit like baking: you do not need to learn chemistry to make a cake, you only have to follow the recipe. For the majority of text-based ebooks, the process is straightforward and easier than you might imagine. You will find, too, that the more you build your own ebooks, the less mysterious HTML becomes. You can even develop your own template code to create consistency in an ebook series, for example, or to streamline the process for your later ebooks.

What You Will Need

A Word Processor

This manual assumes the majority of authors are using **Microsoft Word**. (Although Word is not free, its use is so ubiquitous that to offer instructions for any other word processor would be a disservice to the majority of readers.) Users of **OpenOffice**, **LibreOffice**, **NeoOffice**, **Google Docs** or **Atlantis** can follow the same principles indicated for Word users and export to HTML. With some you also have the option to export to ePub and fix if necessary in Sigil. Same applies to **Apple Pages**, which can export to ePub but not HTML. Users of **Scrivener** will need to export to text and import into a word processor because Scrivener does not support styles (and the ePubs it makes are not industry standard).

Instructions herein refer to Word 2013 for PC. I chose this version because it is neither the latest, which most users rarely have, nor the oldest, which most users have by now abandoned. And if you regularly update your copy of Word, many of the options update as well, so you should easily be able to follow the instructions herein. Earlier versions of Word for PC have equivalent functions, as do Word for Mac and other word processors. Tinker with your program as necessary.

HTML Editor (optional)

If you decide you only want to go the HTML-to-Kindle route, you will need an editor such as Notepad (PC), TextEdit (Mac), or the open-source HTML editor KompoZer. None of these will be necessary if you work in Sigil.

Sigil

Sigil is best downloaded from its official host, GitHub (see links at end of chapter). Sigil can also be found on third-party websites, but I *strongly advise that you do not download from these sites*: they often add malicious code such as adware, or they bundle Sigil with a trial version of another program you don't want or need. Downloading from GitHub also ensures you have the latest release.

Note that you will only need the actual Sigil program, not any of the developer files; you only need the Mac-Package, Windows-Setup, or Windows-X64-Setup file, whichever is appropriate for your system. Note that, as an open-source software, Sigil is updated often as new features are added or bugs are found and fixed. Thus you may find that something has changed slightly from what you see in this manual. If you need further help, there is an excellent forum on the website MobileRead dedicated to Sigil.

ePub Validator

For validating your ePubs, you can use the **online validator at** the **International Digital Publishing Forum (IDPF)**, but I find using **Pagina's** free **EPUB-Checker** to be a quicker and easier solution. Importantly, EPUB-Checker does not require an Internet connection when you use it, and it handles files larger than 10MB, a restriction of the online validator tool.

ePub Apps

For testing ePubs, you can use **Adobe Digital Editions** (ADE) or any of the many other free ePub apps available. I like to use ADE in my computer for initial testing, then I use **Aldiko** for Android on my tablet. I finish with my **Kobo** device and apps. **Apple** computers and tablets have the built-in **iBooks** reader. There are ePub apps for many browsers such as **Firefox** or **Chrome**.

There are a number of ePub apps for smartphones, whether Android or iOS. When choosing which apps to use, make sure ePubs can be sideloaded directly into your phone or downloaded to your device via Dropbox or your Google account, to cite two examples.

Kindle Previewer and Reading Apps

For conversion and testing for Kindle, you will need to download **Kindle Previewer 2.94** from Amazon. At time of writing, Amazon were beta-testing **Kindle Previewer 3**, which includes their Enhanced Typesetting features. I recommend you install both versions on your computer and test in each. You can also download the **Kindle for PC (or Mac) app** and test there. For mobile previews, download the free Kindle app for your phone's operating system.

Kindle Previewer replicates (though not perfectly) the display behaviour of the latest Kindle devices. It will also create a Kindle for iOS file, but you cannot view it in Previewer; it must be sideloaded onto an Apple device. For publishers on PC who do not own an Apple device, you have to go on faith or ask someone with an Apple device to test for you.

eBook devices and apps rarely function identically, even from the same manufacturer. For example, a Kindle device and Amazon's Kindle for PC app do not contain all the same functions and do not display identically. **It is recommended that you test your ebook in as many devices and apps as is possible within your budget.**

Links

Sigil
https://github.com/Sigil-Ebook/Sigil/releases

Adobe Digital Editions
http://www.adobe.com/solutions/ebook/digital-editions/download.html

Kindle Previewer
https://www.amazon.com/gp/feature.html?docId=1000765261

Kindle for PC/Mac
https://www.amazon.com/gp/digital/fiona/kcp-landing-page/ref=kcp_ipad_mkt_lnd

IDPF online validator
http://validator.idpf.org/

Pagina EPUB-Checker
https://github.com/IDPF/epubcheck

Sigil forum on MobileRead.com
https://www.mobileread.com/forums/forumdisplay.php?f=203

All links are valid as of writing but may change in the interim. If so, a quick online search will bring them up.

eBook Development

Ever since the inception of their ebook retail division, and the launch of Kindle Direct Publishing, Amazon have remained committed to developing a proprietary format, the Kindle, and to manufacturing format-specific Kindle devices; the Kindle is thus both an ereader device and a file format. Kindle books have the file extension .azw; the AZW file is a variation of the older mobi file, which is a variation of the PRC file first developed by Mobipocket Creator (which Amazon purchased). Kindle devices and apps will thus read all three files: AZW, mobi, and PRC.

In contrast to Amazon's Kindle, the rest of the tech industry has been primarily devoted to the open-source ePub format, which is sold on all other ebook retail sites outside of Amazon. Very early on the ePub was way ahead of Kindle in terms of features, allowing, for example, the inclusion of embedded fonts, drop caps, colored text, bulleted lists, text boxes, right margin indents and so on that Kindle books did not.

Amazon's response to this was Kindle Format 8 (K8). K8 brought the Kindle into the same league as the ePub, but this created two problems for publishers: 1) older Kindle (mobi7) devices could not read K8 code; and 2) the code produced for these K8 features in programs such as Word was simply incompatible with K8 devices.

Amazon addressed the first issue with media queries—additional code that allows the publisher to create different versions of their ebook in a single file—but such files could not be created by Amazon's auto-conversion process. Publishers whose ebooks required media queries had to learn a new skill or pay an ebook designer.

Amazon have never really addressed the second problem, mainly because they cannot change the code in Word or any other word processor. Instead, Amazon continue to accept text documents for auto-conversion while simultaneously discouraging authors from submitting them, which has resulted in contradictory directions on the KDP website.

The truth is, as Amazon rushed to develop K8, the differences between the proprietary Kindle and the open-source ePub became less and less marked. Now, for text-based ebooks (such as novels), the only real difference between the two formats is a few lines of code.

Where the ePub and Kindle formats do differ dramatically is in image handling. Adding internal images to a Kindle book is far easier than adding them to ePubs. For the typical author self-publishing an ebook with only a cover image, this issue will not arise. **Consequently, I have separated this manual into standard and advanced formatting techniques, saving the more complex but less common techniques for the latter section.**

Because the ePub format is open source, companies are free to modify it as they wish and to use the code as the basis for proprietary formats such as Apple's iBooks Author format or Nook's Kids Book Builder. Device manufacturers also create quirks in their device programming to force publishers to build retailer-specific files, which in turn forces consumer loyalty to a retailer's catalogue and devices. Where applicable these differences are discussed in this manual.

Characteristics of eBooks

An ebook appears on your computer as a single file but it is actually what is known as an archive, a zipped folder containing separate subfolders and files. These subfolders and files contain the ebook's text, images, fonts if embedded, stylesheet(s), and metadata, and to which ebook retailers add code for such things as digital rights management (DRM).

When talking about ebooks, you will always hear references to HTML. HTML is the language of the Internet; it is what web pages are built upon. Another coding language, XML, is a document mark-up language designed for encoding documents intended to be read across the web. XHTML is a combination of the two and is what ebooks are built upon.

There are essentially three types of ebooks on the market now: reflowable, fixed layout, and PDF.

Reflowable eBooks

Reflowable ebooks require different formatting than print books because ebooks do not have fixed margins, page length, or font size. Instead, the font is scalable—meaning the user can adjust the font size on their device to suit their reading preference—and thus there is no fixed placement of the text on the screen; the text simply flows through. Also, each device has a different screen size so you cannot design to a specific digital "page," and some devices allow users to adjust the white margins around the text.

Consequently, in reflowable ebooks there are no page numbers, though some devices can display "page" markers so the ebook can be quoted and properly referenced as a print book can be. Page markers are added by the reading device, so you needn't worry about adding these to your document.

Reflowable ebooks are the preferred format for novels and other text-based ebooks. While reflowable ebooks often contain images, the text is dominant. The majority of self-published authors release reflowable ebooks, of which there are two formats: Kindle and ePub.

The Kindle Format

The older Kindle mobi7 format is all but phased out, and many publishers simply no longer accommodate consumers still using older Kindle devices. That said, there are many still out there, and thus some publishers still use media queries to satisfy these consumers. If you are releasing a novel or similar, media queries will not be necessary. For publishers with more complex ebooks, the code for adding media queries is illustrated in "Advanced Formatting."

As already indicated, Kindle Format 8 allows for more advanced formatting than mobi7. We will thus be focusing on K8, indicating issues with mobi7 only where applicable.

There is a new format, Kindle Format X (Ten; extension .kfx). KFX is a whole new Kindle format, based on Javascript instead of XHTML. Amazon convert existing ebook formats into this new proprietary format, and as such publishers must still produce ePub, mobi, or HTML files, using the formatting found in this manual, for upload to Amazon.

KFX books are not compatible with older mobi7 or mobi8 devices, of which there are literally millions in the hands of consumers. These consumers will have a K8 or mobi7 version of your ebook sent to their devices.

At time of writing, KFX is still in the beta stage and is not being applied equally to all new ebooks because KFX does not yet support all features found in K8. Critics have complained that KFX formatting has been applied—without notification to publishers—to tens of thousands of ebooks already on sale, sometimes with adverse effects. eBooks available in KFX show "Enhanced Typesetting: Enabled" on the ebook's product page.

KFX also includes a new encryption method to prevent Kindle books from being converted to other formats in software such as Calibre (at least until Calibre's developers, and others like them, figure out the code). This applies even to ebooks not DRMed by the publisher. Critics believe this is a strategy to force consumer compliance to Kindle devices and apps.

ePub2 Versus ePub3

The ePubs created by Sigil are the ePub2 format, based on HTML4 and CSS2. ePub3 uses HTML5 and CSS3, the next-generation code. Kindle Previewer (Kindlegen), which converts ePubs to the Kindle format, will accept both ePub2 and ePub3 files but cannot read all ePub3 elements. Uploading ePub3 files to Amazon is therefore not recommended.

For the publisher releasing a reflowable ebook, ePub3 is not required. More importantly, ePub3 devices are backwards compatible but ePub2 devices cannot read ePub3 files. So unless your ebook requires ePub3 code, producing an ePub3 ebook will impede your sales efforts. This manual, like Sigil itself, thus limits itself to ePub2.

Fixed Layout eBooks

Fixed layout ebooks contain static pages where the text and images are fixed and cannot be changed by the end user. Fixed layout ebooks often contain pop-up text boxes, or the reader can zoom in on graphics or text. Some fixed-layout formats can also contain other media such as video or audio files; if so, these are called rich media ebooks. Fixed layout ebooks are the preferred format for image-centric ebooks: comic books, graphic novels, children's books, cookbooks, and some textbooks.

Amazon have developed free software for building fixed layout ebooks for Kindle: Kindle Kids' Book Creator, Kindle Comic Creator, and Kindle Textbook Creator.

Apple's version is the free iBooks Author, a proprietary format (.iba) built on a modified ePub. iBooks Author files can only be built on Apple computers, sold through the Apple iBookstore, and read on Apple devices.

Barnes & Noble have also developed a proprietary children's ebook software, Nook Kids Book Builder, which, like iBooks Author, creates modified ePubs. Children's Nook books can only be sold on B&N and read on Nook devices.

Retailers who have produced software for fixed layout ebooks require that such ebooks be built in their proprietary software or they cannot be sold on the retailer's site. As such, fixed layout ebooks are not covered by this manual.

PDFs

Adobe PDFs have been around for ages, but in the early days of ebooks the PDF format was rejected for its poor quality on the small, low-resolution screens of the early ereaders. With the advent of larger, higher-resolution tablet screens, PDFs are making a comeback for their close proximity to the print book, and are popular with libraries. However, there is not yet wide distribution of PDFs, and most of the major ebook retailers—Amazon, Apple, B&N, Kobo—do not sell the PDF format. As an indie publisher you will likely only encounter the PDF if you opt also to sell a print version of your book or have access to library distribution.

Language Options

Amazon currently accept ebooks published in Afrikaans, Alsatian, Basque, Bokmål Norwegian, Breton, Catalan, Cornish, Corsican, Danish, Dutch/Flemish, Eastern Frisian, English, Finnish, French, Frisian, Galician, German, Icelandic, Irish, Italian, Japanese, Luxembourgish, Manx, Northern Frisian, Norwegian, Nynorsk Norwegian, Portuguese, Provençal, Romansh, Scots, Scottish Gaelic, Spanish, Swedish, and Welsh. eBooks published in other languages will be removed from sale.

The ePub2 format can display any language that is read left to right and horizontal. Right-to-left and vertical languages usually require ePub3 files, and as such are not covered in this manual. And although the ePub format has wider language support than Kindle, not all retailers accept all languages. For example, while Kobo accept most languages, Apple sell only ebooks in English, Arabic, Catalan, Chinese, Croatian, Czech, Danish, Dutch, Finnish, French, German, Greek, Hebrew, Hungarian, Indonesian, Italian, Japanese, Korean, Malay, Norwegian, Polish, Portuguese, Romanian, Russian, Slovak, Spanish, Swedish, Thai, Turkish, Ukrainian, and Vietnamese. If publishing in a "global language" (read: non-Latin alphabet), check first with the retailers you wish to sell through.

An ebook in a global language almost always requires the publisher to embed the necessary font to display all foreign characters correctly. Font embedding is covered in "Advanced Formatting."

1 Format Your Manuscript

Authors who follow these formatting guidelines will create a manuscript that will be much easier to convert to the ePub and Kindle formats, and one that is much less likely to produce common errors that degrade the quality of your ebook.

Most of you will be reading this after you have already written your manuscript. Don't worry: much of what I am writing here can still be applied after the fact. If not, you will be able to fix things later in Sigil. That said, the more you can do to clean up your manuscript before importing into Sigil, the less work you will have later.

Language Settings

In your Word options, under the Language tab (File > Word Options > Language) is the ability to Choose Editing Languages. (You can also access this via Review > Language > Language Preferences.) In the dialogue box that opens you will find the default editing language already installed. The default in copies of Word shipped in North America is "English (United States)". Beneath this is an option to add more editing languages, and a button to set your default editing language from among those specified in the box (Fig. 1.1).

Fig. 1.1

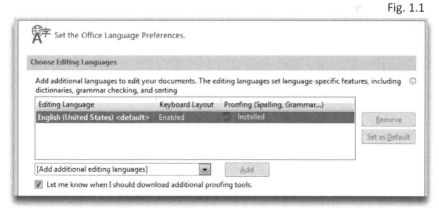

In your Word document itself you have the option to set the proofing language (Review > Set Proofing Language). This sets the default language of the Normal style within your document and, if you choose, the default Word template (Fig. 1.2).

Fig. 1.2

When your Word document is later exported to HTML, in it will be a line of code that states which language your document is written in. **Contrary to logic, this code is determined by the default editing language in your Word options, *not* by the proofing language of your document.** The code will thus always be <body lang=EN-US> if you have a North American version of Word and have never changed the default editing language.

A problem arises if the proofing language of your document differs from your default editing language. If so, then Word creates a formatting override ("inline styling") for the Normal style in your document. Since all ebook styles must be based on the Normal style, this creates an override in *every paragraph of your manuscript*, otherwise known as bloated code. For example, if your editing language is the default U.S. English but your document language is UK English, you will find <span lang=EN-UK> in every paragraph of your document. If you are writing in French you will find <span lang=FR>, and so on for other languages.

When you later build your ebook in Sigil, you will specify your ebook's language in the metadata, which will tell the ereader device what language your ebook is written in. However, both the language code and the inline styling created by Word will remain unless you remove them. The first is easy to delete (it's only one line of code) but the inline styling found in every paragraph will be tedious to remove. While it may not harm your ebook, I'm of the opinion that the cleaner your code the more stable your ebook. So this is best fixed at the outset, and it is easy to do.

To fix the problem, you need to synchronize the primary editing language in your Word options with the proofing language of the Normal style in your document:

    1. First ensure your default editing language in your Word options is the same language your document is written

in. If not, change as appropriate.

2. If you changed the default editing language, close then reopen Word to put the change into effect.

3. Open your manuscript, select all text (Ctrl+A) and set the proofing language to match (even if it was correct to begin with). This will erase from your manuscript code any previous language overrides.

The flip side to this is that **if you use foreign words or phrases in your ebook, you can set the language just for those words or phrases by highlighting them and then selecting Review > Set Proofing Language.** This will create an inline language style just for the select text. If the user then clicks on a foreign word, some ereaders will then open this secondary dictionary instead of the primary language dictionary. The definition will be in the foreign language, too, though—the ereader will not translate— but this mechanism can be useful for multilingual consumers who may simply not be familiar with the foreign word(s) you have used. I am hoping that in future we will see translation dictionaries in ebooks, which will benefit from this technique.

Document Properties

Word offers the option to include in your document metadata your author name, document title, subject, keywords, category, status, and comments; you access this by selecting File > Info. The author name is automatically filled in with the name of the program user (as set in your operating system); **the remaining fields are blank and should be left that way. If not, delete any field entries.**

Document Set-Up

Set your document to a single page size applied to the whole document. Do not split your document into sections that are formatted differently. If you already did this, remove the section breaks.

Page margins are irrelevant, so you may set your margin width as you wish. However, the same margins must be applied to the whole document. If you set different margins partway through your manuscript, you will inadvertently create a section break.

Turn off most AutoCorrect options: File > Proofing > AutoCorrect Options.

Then, under tabs for both/either AutoFormat and AutoFormat As You Type, uncheck: "Automatic bulleted lists", "List Styles", "Ordinals (1st) with superscript", "Border lines", "Automatic numbered lists", "Tables", and "Set left- and first-indent with tabs and backspaces". Left as is, many of these AutoCorrect options will later cause you grief.

There are no page numbers in ebooks, no header or footer information. If you used these in your manuscript, remove them.

You will later use Sigil to build your table of contents. If you used your word processor's table of contents module, or if you built a table of contents by hand, remove it.

The Importance of Using Styles

Most authors who use Word do not use custom styles; instead, authors are in the habit of using the default Normal style then using the tab key and formatting toolbar to create headings or different styles of paragraphs. Unfortunately, not only are tabs not recognized in ebooks, but **the habit of simply overriding the Normal paragraph results in a very poorly coded ebook, one that can be unstable when viewed on different devices.**

When you modify text, the paragraph is still defined by its primary style and then additional information is generated that indicates the changes made. For example, if you modify a line of Normal text to create a chapter heading by increasing the font to 18 points and centering the text, in your Styles window you would find "18pt, Centered" added to your list.

(In older versions of Word, a plus sign [+] is added to the style in use, followed by the modifications made. For example, in the list of styles in use in your document, Normal would be indicated by the ¶ symbol and the modification would appear below it as "Normal+ 18 pt Centered". In newer versions of Word, the plus sign is added only to styles other than Normal.)

The problem with using this method is that such paragraph modifications are translated into inline text styling when you export to HTML, and this inline styling can create havoc in your ebook.

More importantly, ebooks use what is called a Cascading Style Sheet (CSS) to format the different paragraph styles and headings contained within your ebook. When you later convert your manuscript to HTML, the styles you use in your word processor will form the basis of your CSS; if you do not use styles, it will be much more difficult to build your ebook. The sooner you embrace styles the sooner you will be on the road to creating a more professional manuscript and a more beautiful ebook. If you have already finished your manuscript and did not use styles, do not fret: you can create your styles now and then apply them to your text.

Creating Styles

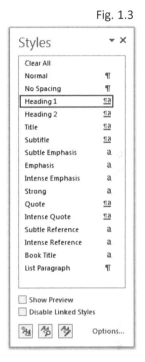

Fig. 1.3

A style is akin to a recipe: it says this style equals whatever combination of font and paragraph formatting you input. Styles can be quite specific to include any possible paragraph formatting from font type and size to paragraph alignment and indentation and Before/After values, and so on. The beauty of styles is that if you later decide to modify your document, you merely have to modify the relevant styles rather than go through your 300-page manuscript. For example, if you have a chapter heading style that has an After value of 24 points and you later think this is too little, you can change the After value in the style to, say, 36 points and every chapter heading that uses that style will automatically be adjusted without affecting other text not based on that style, such as your body text.

Word has a number of default styles, the most obvious one being Normal, but also various default heading styles, a hyperlink style, a footnote style, and so on. You can create your own styles to suit your document or you can modify the default styles.

To modify a default style, click on the Styles submenu on the toolbar to open the Styles dialogue box (Fig. 1.3). In the list that appears, pick the style you want to modify; in this example we are modifying Heading 1. Hover over the ¶ª symbol; it will change to an arrow. Click on the arrow and select Modify from the drop-down menu that appears.

In the Modify Style dialogue box that opens (Fig. 1.4), set your basic attributes: font family (Times New Roman, for example), font size, font style (Bold, Italic), font color (use Automatic for black), paragraph

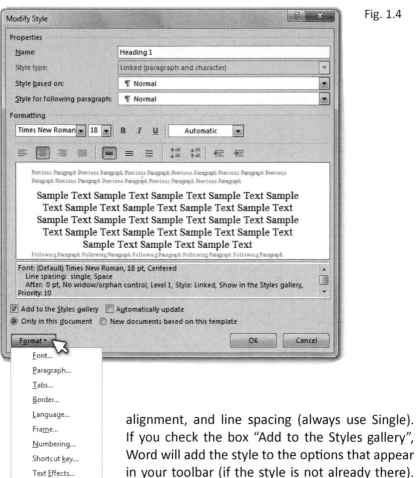

Fig. 1.4

alignment, and line spacing (always use Single). If you check the box "Add to the Styles gallery", Word will add the style to the options that appear in your toolbar (if the style is not already there). Never check "Automatically Update".

Although this initial dialogue box also gives you the option to adjust before/after margins and left/right indents, this is better done in the Paragraph dialogue box. While still in the Modify Style box, click on the Format button in the lower-left corner. A number of options will appear. Click on Paragraph. Here you can adjust the spacing and margin indents, create a first-line indent or hanging paragraphs (Fig. 1.5).

You can also create your own styles. To create a new style, in the Styles box click on the New Style icon (the first of the three icons in the lower-left corner, Fig. 1.3). Input your new style's attributes. **NOTE: all styles must be based on Normal.** Give the style a name and click OK.

Format Your Manuscript • 17

You may find as you reformat your manuscript that it can be very useful to click on the Options button in the lower righthand corner of the Modify Style box and, in the next box that opens, select "In Current Document" under "Select styles to show:" (Fig. 1.6). This reduces the lengthy "All styles" list down to a more manageable one. You will also find it helpful to check the boxes for "Paragraph level formatting" and "Font level formatting" and "Show next heading when previous level is used", and then select "Only in this document". Leave all other options unchecked. Click OK to close.

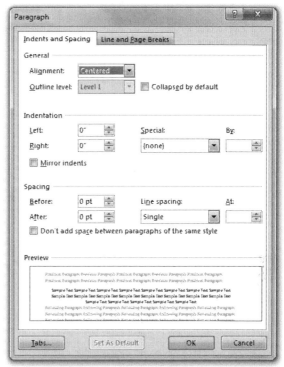

Fig. 1.5 (top) and Fig. 1.6 (bottom)

Applying Styles

To change a paragraph or heading's style, simply place your cursor anywhere in the paragraph or heading and click on the style you wish to change to. This will apply the new style to the paragraph or heading.

If you already used styles in your manuscript, you may find that you only have to make a few changes to your styles in order to accommodate the general formatting principles outlined in this chapter.

If you have not used styles in your manuscript, and you used the Normal paragraph throughout, the quickest route is to modify the Normal style to create a line break (if wanted) or to eliminate issues such as tabs. Then reformat your headings and any special paragraphs. Delete any unwanted line breaks created with a carriage return, and delete any tabs. Both can be quickly accomplished using Search & Replace.

WARNING: If you modify the Normal style to include a first-line indent, remember to remove that indent when you format your heading and other styles.

WARNING: When you convert a paragraph to another style, some versions of Word will erase text effects such as Italic or Bold. Sometimes Italic is erased but Bold remains; other times the formatting remains if only a portion of the paragraph has been modified, while erasing all formatting if the whole paragraph is modified. Sometimes Word will convert the paragraph to the new style but keep an override such as font size even though Word erases every other override. It's a real mishmash. Be mindful of this when converting a paragraph from one style to another.

Heading Styles

Your chapter heading should be created with Heading 1. Your first subheading should be Heading 2, and the subheading of Heading 2 should be Heading 3, and so on. This is because when you later build your table of contents (TOC) in Sigil using its automated module, it is programmed to recognize these headings and will cascade them for you in ascending order:

> (Chapter) Heading 1
>   (Sub) Heading 2
>   (Sub) Heading 3

Sigil allows you to edit the TOC manually, but by using the headings as intended you avoid the work you will otherwise have to do to build your TOC. What I usually do is use Heading 1 for my chapter headings; if I want to format other page headings such as Acknowledgements, About the Author, and so on, differently from my chapter heading, I use a different style and then manually add these entries to my TOC later in Sigil.

WARNING: Do not use Heading styles on your title page. If the end user turns off publisher formatting (discussed in more detail in the next chapter), most ereader apps are programmed to treat any Heading 1 and

Heading 2 entries as chapter headings and may add a page break before them.

Character Styles

Character styles can be created in the same way as paragraph styles: open the Styles box and click on the New Style button to open the options box. Give the style a name, and in the field beneath, Style Type, open the drop-down menu and select Character. You will then see that paragraph formatting options are grayed out, leaving you only font options to choose from.

To apply a character style, highlight the relevant text and then click on the style.

WARNING: Never create a character style that involves changing the font size. For inexplicable reasons, Word creates the style but then uses inline styling for the font size. It makes no sense, and you will just have to fix the mess later in Sigil. If you want to create a character style that changes the font size, you will have to do it later in Sigil. This is covered in "Advanced Formatting."

WARNING: Do not use a character style to create drop caps. Drop caps must be built by hand later in Sigil: the code Word creates does not display properly in ebooks. Drop caps are covered in "Advanced Formatting."

Emphasis and Strong

Two default character styles in Word that you may find useful are Emphasis and Strong. Emphasis by default italicizes the text, and Strong bolds the text. However, they create different code than Italic or Bold, and this code is interpreted by Text-to-Speech (TTS) software differently than Italic and Bold. TTS software is used to read your ebook aloud to the user, though few ebook devices have this option. (Some older Kindles do, and there are apps available for Windows, Android, and iOS.)

In theory, Emphasis (`<em>`) tells the TTS reader to emphasize the text, as in "Get out—*Now!*"; Italic (`<i>`) is used for foreign words, interior dialogue, titles of books, and so on, and is read in a normal tone.

Similarly, Strong (`<strong>`) is used to bold text and is pronounced more forcefully by the TTS editor than Emphasis. You might use it, for example, in "The sign said '**Danger—Keep Out!**'"

Now, I say "in theory" for two reasons: 1) some TTS software is programmed to emphasize all italicized text, which defeats your efforts; and 2) in HTML5, `<strong>` no longer means "strong emphasis" but now simply means "important". So it all depends on how the TTS software is programmed. That said, it certainly doesn't hurt to put in the code for those TTS readers that are programmed as expected.

Emphasis and Strong (or Bold) can be used together to create emphasized Bold Italic text. They can also be further controlled through classes when you create your ebook in Sigil. This is covered in "Advanced Formatting."

Fonts

When you export to HTML, and your styles are translated into CSS, each style will specify which font you used for that style; this is called a font-family attribute. However, ebook devices are limited in the fonts they have installed, no two devices have the same fonts installed, and thus most are not able to display the font your code indicates. The result is that ebooks have been developed based on the user selecting which font they wish to read your ebook in, chosen from among their device's or app's options, rather than the font you wrote your book in.

Amazon no longer want font-family attributes included at all in Kindle files because this can interfere with the user's ability to choose their preferred font. **Consequently, regardless of which font you use, you will delete this information when you build your ebook. Choosing a font for its look is therefore pointless.** With ePubs the same principle applies.

For ease of use, **I format my manuscripts in Times New Roman** because it contains recognized text effects and the Windows-1252 character set, both discussed below.

If it is essential that your ebook display more than one font, or a specific font, that font can be embedded in your ebook. Font embedding is covered in "Advanced Formatting."

Text Effects

Digital devices in general will recognize Italic, Bold, Superscript, Subscript, and Strike-through text effects. All other text effects cannot be read and will be converted to Regular text. This includes Double Strike-through, Shadow, Outline, Emboss, Engrave, Small Caps, All Caps, Hidden Text, Horizontal Scaling, Raised Text, and Lowered Text.

Underline is now a special case as the code for it (<u>) has been deprecated (rendered obsolete) in ePub code. To create underlined text you now must create a character style. Creating a new character style for Underline is covered in "Advanced Formatting."

(Although the code for Underline will still be read by pretty much every ereader out there, using <u> will cause your ePub to fail validation, an essential step to putting your ebook on sale.)

If you need underlined text that will not easily be found without later digging through your manuscript line by line, use Word's Underline feature for now so as to create an easily found bit of code, but know that it will have to be replaced later.

Both Superscript and Subscript will cause odd line spacing in ebooks, and thus the trend is to use them only when necessary, such as in mathematical concepts. So instead of writing "1st" one simply writes "1st". If you have an AutoCorrect option set to change ordinals to superscript, I recommend you turn it off.

Text Characters

Amazon have focused on languages that use the Latin alphabet. This is why you will find on the Kindle Direct Publishing website a directive to use only Latin-1 characters. This is actually a bit misleading since **Kindle books will in fact read all characters found in the Windows-1252 character set** (Fig. 1.7), which incorporates Latin-1 and also the subsets Basic Latin, General Punctuation, and a handful of characters from Latin Extended-B. Windows-1252 is also known as Western European (Windows).

Fig. 1.7

```
0 1 2 3 4 5 6 7 8 9 - = [ ] \ ; ' , . / ` ~ ! @ # $ % ^ & * ( ) _ + { } | :
" < > ? A B C D E F G H I J K L M N O P Q R S T U V W X Y Z a b c
d e f g h I j k l m n o p q r s t u v w x y z ¡ ¢ £ ¤ ¥ ¦ § ¨ © ª « ¬ - ®
¯ ° ± ² ³ ´ µ ¶ · ¸ ¹ º » ¼ ½ ¾ ¿ À Á Â Ã Ä Å Æ Ç È É Ê Ë Ì Í Î Ï Ð Ñ Ò
Ó Ô Õ Ö × Ø Ù Ú Û Ü Ý Þ ß à á â ã ä å æ ç è é ê ë ì í î ï ð ñ ò ó ô
õ ö ÷ ø ù ú û ü ý þ ÿ ‹ ›
€ , ƒ „ … † ‡ ^ ‰ Š ‹ Œ Ž ' ' " " • – — ~ ™ š › œ ž Ÿ ¡
```

As stated at the start of this manual, ePubs can read many global languages but usually only if the font is embedded. This is because the fonts licensed by device manufacturers rarely include global language characters and are thus unable to display non-Latin languages correctly.

eReaders and apps can also read some Unicode characters, though how many characters varies greatly.

Font embedding and Unicode are covered in "Advanced Formatting." For now we will restrict ourselves to Windows-1252.

Symbols and Subsets

You can use symbols only if they belong to the Windows-1252 character set. In Word, if you select Insert > Symbol, in the box that appears you will see on the left the Font field (the default is "(normal text)") and on the right the Subset field (Fig. 1.8). In the Subset drop-down menu you will find such subsets as Basic Latin, Latin-1, Latin-1 Supplement, Latin Extended-A, IPA Extensions, and so on. However, as indicated, only those characters found in Windows-1252 will be recognized by all ereaders. **A simple way to make sure you are using only the allowed characters is to change the default "Unicode (hex)" option in the "from" field to "ASCII (decimal)"**; when you do this you will notice the Subset field disappears, and now you will only be shown the Windows-1252 character set.

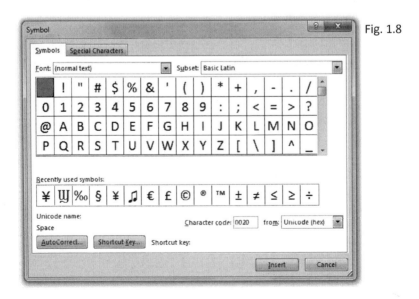

Fig. 1.8

Fractions can be written as either Normal text (1/2) or as symbols (½), but keep in mind that the latter will be harder to read on the digital screen than the former.

WARNING: When you insert a symbol, make sure the Font field is set to "(normal text)". This ensures you do not inadvertently create an inline font style in your Word code that you will later have to clean out.

Font Color

For black text, use only Word's Automatic font coloring. Using Black will result in a text color inline style that will later have to be removed.

Amazon state that body text should not have an imposed color; however, different colors for headings and special sections are allowed. Adding color to text is covered in "Advanced Formatting."

Font Size

Although you set your font size in points in Word, those points will be changed to ems when you build your ebook. An em is the width of the letter *m*, and varies with the design and size of the font. In ereaders, the base value of em is set by the device. Thus a font size of 1em will look larger or smaller on different devices, or a different size in a different font.

Kindle Direct Publishing and others require a body text size of 1em. All other text—headings, subheadings, endnotes, et cetera—are then set in relation to your body text. I therefore set my body text to 10 points in my Word manuscript, while a chapter heading might be 20 points and the text on my copyright page might be 9 points. **I then later use a simple system of 10pt = 1em to convert.**

As the user increases the font size in their device, the device tries to maintain the ratio between your different font sizes. For example, if your body text is 1em and your chapter heading is 2em, the ratio between heading and body text is 2:1. Some ereaders will maximize the font size when the *largest* font in your document reaches the device's limit, maintaining some semblance of the 2:1 ratio. Other devices will maximize the font size when the *smallest* font in your document reaches the device's limit; in this case the 2:1 ratio becomes increasingly reduced until no difference exists and all text displays at the same size.

For the most part you needn't worry about this because only those users with severe visual restrictions will ever set their ereader to its maximum font size; most users set their screen font to what one would likely find in a print book. When you later check your ebook, test at a normal font size to determine if the look of the ebook is satisfactory.

Character Spacing

Do not use character spacing to create more pleasing text alignment as one does in a print book, or to widen heading text for example. Character spacing is not recognized by most ereaders, and in some devices it can cause the text to display at the default size (so your heading will be reduced to body text size). In general, it is best to leave all character spacing at its default 100% scale, Normal spacing, and Normal position (Style > Modify > Format > Font > Advanced tab).

WARNING: Some of Word's default Heading styles use expanded character spacing. This must be changed to the defaults outlined above.

Cutting and Pasting

If you cut and paste between documents or from a variety of sources, you will save yourself a lot of later grief if you "scrub" the text before pasting into your document. Doing so ensures hidden code is not inadvertently imported with the text. **This is particularly important if you cut and paste anything from a website.**

Whenever you paste anything into a Word document, a small box appears with a clipboard icon and "(Ctrl)" beside it. This is a drop-down menu that offers three options: 1) Keep Source Formatting; 2) Merge Formatting; or 3) Keep Text Only. **Always choose Keep Text Only as this removes all original formatting.**

Blank Lines and Line Breaks

If you insert blank lines in your document by using carriage returns, these empty lines may be erased by some ereaders. **It is best to incorporate blank lines into a paragraph style using the Before/After spacing option.**

For example, if you want the equivalent of a blank line between paragraphs when using a 10-point font, set the After option to 10pt. If you want two lines, set it to 20pt, and so on. Note that some ePub and Kindle devices/apps do not read the Before spacing; it can be better to use only After spacing.

The exception to this is chapter headings and book titles. If you want them to fall partway down the screen (mimicking the lowered chapter heading in a print book), you can use the Before spacing as well. In ereaders that cannot read the Before spacing, your chapter heading or title will simply rise to the top of the screen but the After spacing will still display.

Do not use carriage returns to break up lines of text so they appear more pleasing to the eye on the page in your word processor. If you do this, the text will reflow in the ereader but the carriage returns will be honoured, and you will end up with a mess. Use a carriage return only at the end of a paragraph.

Soft Return

If you need only the occasional blank line between paragraphs, you can insert one using the soft return (Shift+Enter). This adds a line break but does so by treating the line break as part of the existing paragraph. **You can use the soft return anywhere you need to break up text into separate lines without treating each line as a new paragraph.** If you were then to look at the hidden characters in your Word document, the soft return is represented by an arrow bending backward (in contrast to the hard return, symbolized by ¶).

The Non-Breaking Space Character (NBSP)

The non-breaking space character (Ctrl+Shift+Space) is used anywhere you need to prevent a line break, or to create multiple consecutive spaces in your document. For example, you have a list where you want two or more spaces between the number and the list item ("1: Item one"), or you want to prevent a compound noun like *72 ppi* from splitting over two lines. You may be writing poetry and need deliberate spaces between words ("The space   between us"). Or you need to create blank spaces at the start of a line where a first-line indent may be problematic. The only way to create these additional spaces properly is by using the non-breaking space character instead of a regular space.

When you click on the ¶ sign on your Word toolbar to view hidden characters, the NBSP appears in your text as the degrees sign (°). So "72 ppi" would appear as "72°ppi".

In addition to creating a space, the NBSP, as its name suggests, prevents the words or characters it connects from breaking over to the next line on the screen, so **you must be careful to use the NBSP sparingly as it can cause odd text alignment.**

Page Breaks

Do not add page breaks to your document using Word's Insert > Page Break option. In fact, page breaks of any kind in your manuscript are not necessary because you will later create these in Sigil using proper ebook techniques.

Similarly, **do not use carriage returns to force text onto the next page,** such as at the start of a chapter. Such carriage returns will cause problems for you later.

Dashes

If using an en dash (–) or em dash (—), whether you separate the dash from the surrounding text is now a matter of taste. However, if you use spaces around your dashes, it can be preferable to attach the dash to the preceding text using an NBSP. This prevents the dash from falling to and opening the next line, which can jar the reader. **Never use an NBSP to attach the dash to the text that follows.** If you have added your NBSP correctly, you will see "your text°— your text".

That said, **attaching the dash to the preceding text can cause odd text alignment in ereaders.** You really cannot win as you can with print books, so you have to pick your evil. Note that this odd text alignment tends to be more of a problem with smaller screens like mobile phones, or if the user chooses a large screen font. Both are out of your control.

Ellipses

For an ellipsis, you have two options: 1) three periods separated by spaces and held together with NBSPs; or 2) the ellipsis symbol (Alt+Ctrl+.), which is three dots combined into a single character. **You cannot use the third option—three periods with no spaces—because ereaders cannot distinguish that as an ellipsis and may split the periods over two lines.**

The first option creates a look more consistent with print books and tends to create more pleasing character alignment in ereaders. The second option, because it is a single character, cannot be accidentally broken over two lines; however, it can cause odd text alignment. Nevertheless,

I have moved over the years from the first option to the second simply because it is easier and more predictable.

If you use the traditional convention of not separating the ellipsis from the surrounding text ("text…text"), this can cause large white spaces to appear in lines of text because the whole of the *text…text* is read as one word. This affects kerning (the spaces between words and their individual characters).

However, if you separate the ellipsis from the surrounding text, it is recommended you attach the ellipsis to the preceding text with an NBSP; otherwise the ellipsis can fall to the start of the next line. Again, pick your evil.

WARNING: In Word's AutoCorrect (File > Options > Proofing > AutoCorrect Options > AutoCorrect, in the "Replace text as you type" field is the option to automatically replace three periods, no spaces, with the ellipsis symbol. I have worked on many manuscripts where the author had this option on for part of the manuscript and off in others. This creates two different types of ellipses in a single document. Always check for this in your manuscript and fix any inconsistencies.

Footnotes

If you create footnotes in your Word document, when exported to HTML the footnotes are moved to the end of your document into one page of endnotes. The footnote reference link (the number) is turned into a colored hyperlink. When the user wishes to read a footnote, they click on the footnote reference link and are taken to the endnote in the document; to return to their place in the text they merely have to click the back button on their device or click on the footnote number. (Some newer devices use pop-up windows instead.)

Most word processors have a function whereby you can start each section's footnotes at "1", so you can have footnote 1 in chapter 1 and footnote 1 in chapter 2. But as stated earlier, you must not use sections in an ebook document. Thus, **your footnotes should not be numbered per section or chapter, but rather numbered sequentially from start of document to end.** If you do not do so, when you later convert to HTML, any sectioning will be ignored and footnotes will be renumbered anyway into one sequential list based on order of appearance in the manuscript. This might cause you confusion later when you are checking your references for errors.

Footnote Reference Links

Footnote reference links should be left as Regular text because they are automatically hyperlinked and therefore display in a different text color in an ereader. The default style for footnote links—Superscript—can display very small on some ereaders, making it difficult for the user to tap on the link; using a Regular font style solves this problem. Many ebook devices add square brackets around footnote links, further differentiating them.

To change Word's default footnote formatting, you need to modify the Footnote Reference style.

Internal Hyperlinks

In an ebook you can create internal hyperlinks that allow the user to jump to a graphic or to a place in the text and then return to their previous place using their device's back button.

Internal hyperlinks are easier to create in Sigil than in Word, and Word uses code that will later have to be modified in Sigil. If you have not already created internal links in your Word document, save this task for when you build your ebook in Sigil.

Miscellaneous Formatting Principles

Use only the default single line spacing. Many ereaders allow the user to change the line spacing; consequently, Amazon will reject any ebooks in which the line height of the body text is fixed.

Do not use tabs anywhere in your document. If you need to indent the first line of any paragraph, create an appropriate style. It doesn't matter what size of first-line indent you use as you will later change it to a percentage when you convert your manuscript into an ebook.

If you need to indent whole paragraphs, create a style for this. ePubs and K8/KFX devices can display both left- and right-margin indents. Older mobi7 Kindles can only display the left indent and will simply ignore the right indent.

Cascading (multilevel) indents will display in ePubs and K8 devices but will convert to a single-level indent in mobi7 devices. If you want cascading indents to display in older Kindle devices, you can later create alternate code using media queries and blockquotes; instructions for these are included in "Advanced Formatting."

Hanging paragraphs will display as intended in ePub and K8 devices. Mobi7 devices will convert hanging paragraphs to block paragraphs.

Do not use Word's automatic bullets and lists. Create these manually instead using paragraph styles and a recognized bullet symbol, number or asterisk from the Windows-1252 character set. Do not use tabs. In the alternative, use HTML ordered/unordered list code, covered in "Advanced Formatting."

Do not use text columns, frames, tables, or lines. These must be added manually later in Sigil. If you have text that needs to be set in a column, frame, or table, mark it so you can find it easily later and modify then. Columns, frames, tables, and lines are covered in "Advanced Formatting."

Do not manually add hyphenation to create more pleasing paragraph alignment. Use hyphens only where the word itself is hyphenated, as in *self-publishing*. Many ereaders will automatically hyphenate the text to create more pleasing text alignment, though they vary dramatically in their ability to do this properly; for example, you may find *until* hyphenated as *unt-il*. There is nothing you can do about that.

Use only a single space between sentences. The convention of a double space between sentences arose from the days of typewriters and is not appropriate for digital text. More importantly, Sigil will turn one-half of any double space into an NBSP, which you definitely do not want here. Clean out any inadvertent double spaces. I use Word's Find and Replace to rid my manuscript of unwanted spaces.

Clean out spaces before carriage returns. Since a space is required between a period and the start of the next sentence, many of us have a habit of adding in that space when we come to the end of a paragraph and before we hit Enter. These spaces will be turned into an NBSP by Sigil and are read as characters of text. This can cause odd text alignment or can be pushed forward to the next line, creating unwanted blank lines. You can check for unnecessary spaces by clicking on the Show/Hide icon (¶) on your toolbar to view hidden characters, then delete these redundant spaces. Again, I use Word's Find and Replace to do this quickly.

Save as Web Page, Filtered

Once you have finished formatting your manuscript, you need to Save as Web Page, Filtered. To do so, choose File > Save As, and in the "Save as type" drop-down menu select "Web Page, Filtered (*.htm; *html)" (Fig. 1.9). Before you click on Save, click on Tools > Web Options. In the box that opens, select the Encoding tab. Under "Save this document as" select "Unicode (UTF-8)" (Fig. 1.10). Click OK to close the box. Click Save in your main box.

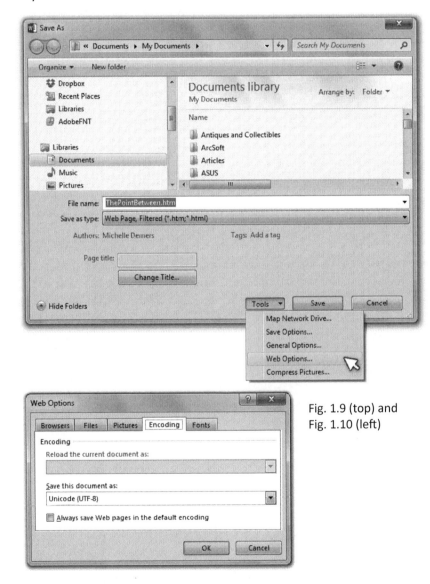

Fig. 1.9 (top) and
Fig. 1.10 (left)

A box will pop up warning you that saving in this manner will remove Office-specific tags. As this is exactly what you want, click Yes. Your Word document will close and the HTML document will open in Word. Close it down.

When you Save as Web Page, Filtered, Word exports your document to HTML and creates a new file that uses the file extension .htm.

WARNING: Make sure you save your manuscript prior to saving to HTML because Word will close down your document *without saving it first*. If you have not saved your final edits, they will be lost in your Word doc but will be there in the HTML version.

WARNING: When naming your document do not use blank spaces. Either eliminate any blank spaces or use the underline ("MyBook.htm" or "My_Book.htm" but not "My Book.htm").

MAC USERS: The Save as Web Page, Filtered option does not exist in Mac. Instead you must Save to Web Page and select "Save only display information into HTML" in the Save dialogue box, which achieves the same effect as Save as Web Page, Filtered.

MAC USERS: You may find that saving as UTF-8 can cause issues with some characters. If you find this is so when importing into Sigil, save your Word doc as HTML but select Western (Windows Latin 1) encoding instead.

NOTE: When you save a document as HTML, three specific characters are converted to their XML equivalent so as not to interfere with the HTML code. These are the less-than sign (<), the greater-than sign (>), and the ampersand (&). While they will appear unchanged when you look at your text, in the code they will be replaced with their XML equivalent.

2 Build Your eBook

You are now ready to build your ebook in Sigil. For the purpose of illustration, I will be converting a file called The Point Between.htm.

In this section I will often bold a line of code to draw attention to it; this is for illustrative purposes only; you will never see Bold text in code. Also note that some longer lines of code will wrap to fit the page here. Depending on the size of your Sigil window, the code may or may not wrap there as well.

As you work through your file, remember to save your work periodically so as not to lose it. That said, if you make an error and then try to save, Sigil will warn you that your file is not well formatted and will offer to fix it but with the caveat that doing so may cause a loss of data (Fig. 2.1).

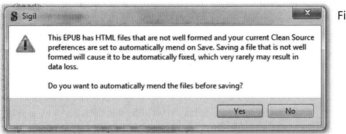

Fig. 2.1

If that happens, I always prefer to choose No and try to figure out what I did wrong before trying to save again. I learn more this way, and often the problem is something as simple as forgetting the forward slash in a closing tag. If you choose Yes, Sigil will fix your file but you won't know what it had to do to fix the problem, which may or may not be an issue later. Choose Yes only if you are really stuck.

NOTE: When following the instructions in this manual, pay attention to uppercase versus lowercase letters. If the spelling of classes in your CSS and your HTML do not match *exactly*, then your code will not work.

Step 1: Import Your HTML File Into Sigil

Open your HTML (.htm) file in Sigil. You can do this by dragging the file onto the Sigil icon on your desktop or by opening Sigil and using the Open

File option. If you use the latter option, in the file type drop-down list in the bottom-right corner, change the default "EPUB files (*.epub)" either to "All files (*.*)" or "HTML files (*.htm, *.html, *.xhtm)".

To look at your HTML file in Sigil you have three options: Code View (Fig. 2.2), Book View (Fig. 2.3), and a handy split-screen version (F10) that allows you to see the results immediately while you edit the code. (Note: Sigil's developers are toying with the idea of removing Book View. If that happens use F10.) In Book View you will notice that at this stage it appears as if all your formatting has been lost. Don't panic: nothing has been lost.

Fig. 2.2 (top) and 2.3 (bottom)

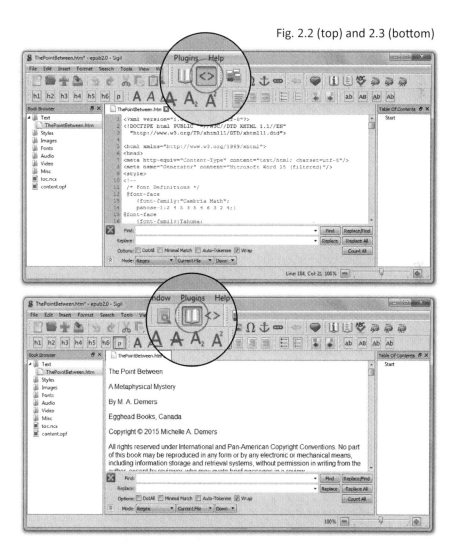

By default, the Sigil window includes the Table of Contents frame on the right side. To maximize the view of the code and content, you can close the TOC frame (click on the *X* at the top-right corner).

Change the File Extension

In the Book Browser frame (left), right-click on your HTML (.htm) document and select Rename (Ctrl+Alt+R) (Fig. 2.4). Change the file extension from .htm to .xhtml.

Header Code

Click on the <> icon to return to Code View. At the top of your document you will find:

```
<?xml version="1.0" encoding="utf-8"?>
<!DOCTYPE html PUBLIC "-//W3C//DTD XHTML 1.1//EN"
"http://www.w3.org/TR/xhtml11/DTD/xhtml11.dtd">
<html xmlns="http://www.w3.org/1999/xhtml">
<head>
```

This is created by Sigil when you import your HTML file. **Never delete or in any way modify this code.**

Fig. 2.4

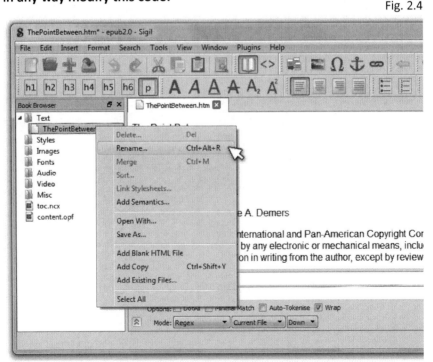

Word Meta Entries

Below `<head>` you will find:

```
<meta http-equiv="Content-Type" content="text/
html; charset=utf-8"/>
<meta name="Generator" content="Microsoft Word 15
(filtered)"/>
```

These two lines of code are created by Word. They are useless for the purpose of an ebook and should be deleted. (Note: the version of Word you are using will be reflected here and will not necessarily be Word 15.)

Step 2: Delete Font Definitions

Below `<head>` is `<style>` (blue text) and then, in green text:

```
/* Font Definitions */
@font-face
{font-family:Tahoma;
panose-1:2 11 6 4 3 5 4 4 2 4;}
```

Which font definitions Word exports in your document seem to be completely arbitrary, and instead of Tahoma you may see other fonts listed. In most cases you will only see a few definitions, but in some versions of Word, for reasons I do not understand, Word exports a font definition *for every font on your computer*, not just those used in your document. This can create literally hundreds of lines of useless code.

You need to delete everything from `/* Font Definitions */` down to the end of your last font definition, which will be right above `/* Style Definitions */` (see highlighted text in Fig. 2.5). If you are one of the unfortunates with hundreds of font definitions, this will mean deleting hundreds of lines of code.

Step 3: Create Your Stylesheet

On the left of the Sigil screen, under Book Browser, right-click on the Styles folder and choose Add Blank Stylesheet. A new tab called Style0001.css will open. Leave it open but click back on your main book tab.

Just below `<head>` you will now see:

```
<style>
<!--
   /* Style Definitions */
```

Fig. 2.5

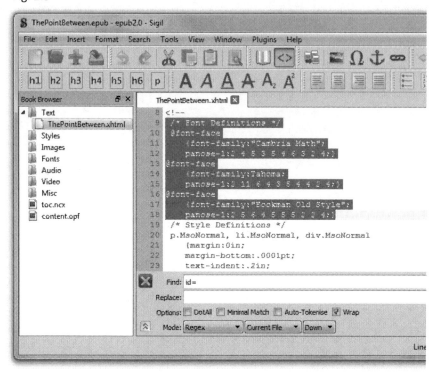

NOTE: in older versions of Word you may find this instead:

```
/*<![CDATA[*/
<!--
    /* Style Definitions */
```

This will be followed by all your style definitions beginning with:

```
p.MsoNormal, li.MsoNormal, div.MsoNormal
```

Select everything from `<style>` (or `/*<![CDATA[*/`) all the way down to `</style>` (Fig. 2.6). Select Edit > Cut (Ctrl+X). Click on the Style0001.css tab. Select Edit > Paste (Ctrl+V).

Under Book Browser, right-click on your XHTML file and select Link Stylesheets… In the box that opens, check "../Styles/Stylesheet001.css". Click OK (Fig. 2.7).

NOTE: If you have any style overrides or character styles, a list of span classes will also be present in your CSS. Depending on your word processor or which version of Word you use, these amendments may be

Build Your eBook • 37

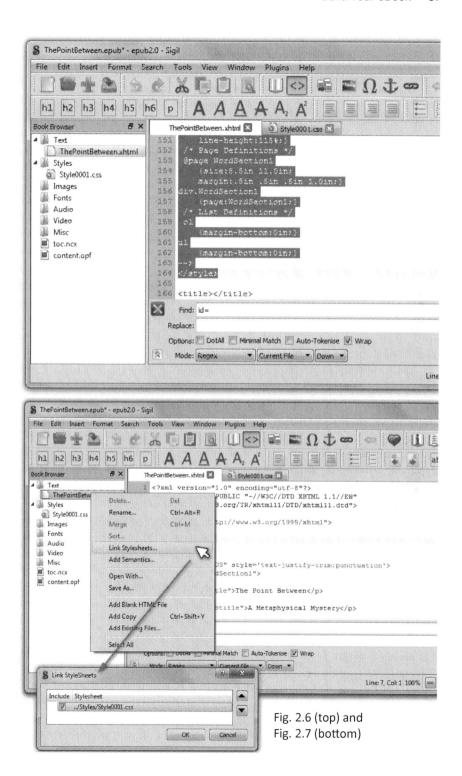

Fig. 2.6 (top) and
Fig. 2.7 (bottom)

interspersed with the list of styles or may be listed together below the primary list of styles. If they are the latter you may find this in the middle:

```
-->
/*]]>*/
</style>
<style type="text/css">
/*<![CDATA[*/
```

If so, you need to include *all* these amendments, in which case you need to scroll down past this code to the *second* `</style>`.

If you now click back on your book tab and click on Book View, you will see that your text formatting has appeared. It won't be perfect yet, but it will be there.

If you did everything correctly, at the top of your document window you will now see your header code looks like this:

```
<head>
<title></title>
<link href="../Styles/Style0001.css" type="text/css" rel="stylesheet"/>
</head>
```

NOTE: You will likely need to delete blank lines left behind when you cut out your CSS.

Step 4: Clean Up Your Stylesheet

Word makes for sloppy CSS, which is one reason why it rarely auto-converts well into the XHTML of ebooks (and why it is not recommended to upload an unedited HTML file to Amazon or others for conversion). The next order of business, then, is to clean up the mess.

Click back on the Style001.css tab. At the top you will find and delete:

```
<style>
<!--
   /* Style Definitions */
```

If your older version of Word created

```
/*<![CDATA[*/
<!--
   /* Style Definitions */
```

and
```
    -->
    /*]]>*/
    </style>
    <style type="text/css">
    /*<![CDATA[*/
```
delete these instead.

Scroll down to the bottom. Find and delete:
```
    /* Page Definitions */
    @page WordSection1
       {size:8.5in 11.0in;
    margin:.5in .5in .5in 1.0in;}
    div.WordSection1
       {page:WordSection1;}
    /* List Definitions */
    ol
       {margin-bottom:0in;}
    ul
       {margin-bottom:0in;}
    -->
    </style>
```

NOTE: Your page size and margins will reflect how you set up your document and may not match mine. As you work through the HTML that follows here, values will vary depending on how you defined your own styles. The principles of the coding, however, will remain the same.

NOTE: In HTML, Word prefixes all its default styles with "Mso" (Microsoft Office). Styles you created yourself will not have this prefix.

As you work through your CSS, you will notice a pattern in the color coding that Sigil uses: a class (that is, the name of the style definition) is red, attributes are blue, and values are black, as are the opening and closing brackets.

If you make a mistake, the color of the code will be incorrect; this is the clue as to where you erred. If you accidentally delete an opening bracket, all your attributes and values turn red like the class name. Delete a closing bracket and the next class turns blue when it should be red. Delete the semicolon after a value and the next attribute is black instead of blue. **Use the colors to guide you and you can easily find and fix a mistake.**

Span Style Links

When Word exports to HTML, the first entry in the CSS is `MsoNormal`, followed by the headings. The first heading you will see is Heading 1 (`h1`).

For certain default Word styles such as headings, in the first line of the style definition Word automatically creates a style link that adds further formatting (why Word does it in this convoluted way is yet another Microsoft mystery). In this case we are looking at Heading 1:

```
h1
    {mso-style-link:"Heading 1 Char";
    margin-top:24.0pt;
    margin-right:0in;
    margin-bottom:24.0pt;
    margin-left:0in;
    text-align:center;
    font-size:18.0pt;
    font-family:"Times New Roman","serif";}
```

If you then scroll down to find the Heading 1 Char style that is linked—

```
span.Heading1Char
    {mso-style-name:"Heading 1 Char";
    mso-style-link:"Heading 1";
    font-family:"Times New Roman","serif";
    font-weight:bold;}
```

—you will see that the only new information is `font-weight:bold`. This is because in this case I added Bold to the default heading style. Cut `font-weight:bold;` from the span style and paste it into the `h1` style definition, and delete `mso-style-link` in h1:

```
h1
    {margin-top:24.0pt;
    margin-right:0in;
    margin-bottom:24.0pt;
    margin-left:0in;
    text-align:center;
    font-size:18.0pt;
    font-weight:bold;
    font-family:"Times New Roman","serif";}
```

Many of these default style links are pointless. For example, I used Word's default Title style, which I modified to suit my document. But I added no special formatting like Bold, and as such the span style link merely circles back on itself:

```
span.TitleChar
  {mso-style-name:"Title Char";
  mso-style-link:Title;}
```

Therefore, there is nothing to add to the Title style; in this case I merely deleted the `mso-style-name` in `MsoTitle`.

Check any other style definitions for which Word created a style link and which you recognize as used in your document (for example, `MsoTitle`, `MsoSubtitle`); if additional formatting is in the style link, cut and paste as you did for `h1`.

Delete Unused Style Definitions

For inexplicable reasons, Word keeps a record of every font and formatting option you used in your document even if you later erase all instances of their use from your manuscript. Word often then exports these unused style definitions, along with several default styles exported for reasons only Microsoft understands. For example, in my HTML file I found styles such as `p.MsoTitleCxSpFirst`, `p.MsoTitleCxSpMiddle`, `p.MsoAcetate`, and so on. All pointless.

The other thing that Word does is create a line (`li`) and division (`div`) class for every paragraph style you created. So instead of just `p.MsoNormal`, you also get `li.MsoNormal` and `div.MsoNormal`. Both equally useless.

Although, technically speaking, unused styles will not do your ebook any harm, I find it helpful to remove these unneeded styles: it makes the stylesheet that much easier to understand and navigate.

Luckily, Sigil has a handy module whereby it will eliminate any unused styles from your CSS. From the toolbar select Tools > Delete Unused Stylesheet Classes. A window will open with all the unused styles that Sigil finds (Fig. 2.8).

Here you will see the redundant line and division classes, and all the unused paragraph and span classes. All are checked by default. Scroll down to the bottom of the list and click on Delete Marked Styles. (If the list is lengthy, you may find that you have to do this twice to get rid of everything.)

What you now have left is a very clean CSS that you can further modify.

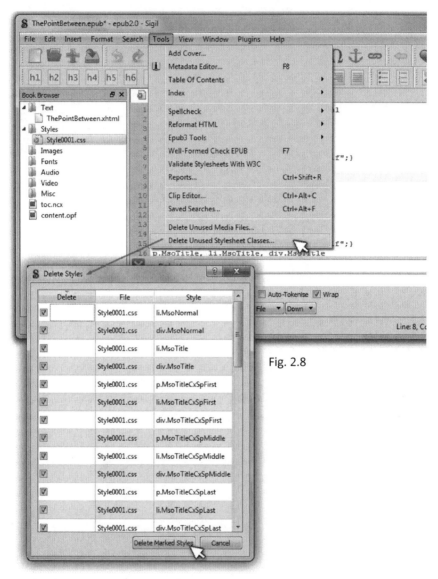

Fig. 2.8

WARNING: Do not do this before you fix the character links discussed in Span Style Links. Otherwise you will have to add any font formatting back in.

Delete Mso-Style-Name (optional)

For styles you create, Word adds the style's name to the first line of the style definition. This is redundant. It won't harm your ebook to leave them in, but you can remove them (I do). For example:

```
p.First
   {mso-style-name:First;
   margin:0in;
   text-indent:0in;
   font-size:10.0pt;}
```

becomes

```
p.First
   {margin:0in;
   text-indent:0in;
   font-size:10.0pt;}
```

Remove Font-Family Attributes

In every style definition you will find the font-family attribute. As we noted in the previous chapter, Amazon and most ePub retailers want this font-family information deleted. Delete every instance of font-family information in your stylesheet. For example:

```
h1
   {margin-top:24.0pt;
   margin-right:0in;
   margin-bottom:24.0pt;
   margin-left:0in;
   text-align:center;
   font-size:18.0pt;
   font-weight:bold;
   font-family:"Times New Roman","serif";}
```

becomes

```
h1
   {margin-top:24.0pt;
   margin-right:0in;
   margin-bottom:24.0pt;
   margin-left:0in;
   text-align:center;
   font-size:18.0pt;
   font-weight:bold;}
```

TIP: I find it useful to use Sigil's Find and Replace module to remove or change multiples of the same value. Here you can copy the font-family attribute into the Find field at the bottom of the Sigil window, then leave the Replace field blank. Below that you will see three Mode fields; in the middle you will see one with the default value of "All HTML Files". From the drop-down menu select "Current File".This will limit the changes to the current Style001.css file.

WARNING: When you delete the final value in a style definition, ensure that you delete only up to the semicolon, leaving the closing bracket (}) intact. If you delete the closing bracket you will break your CSS.

Delete Bottom Margin in MsoNormal

In some versions of Word you will find that if you set the Normal style's bottom margin to 0, a value of .0001pt is nevertheless added in the CSS:

```
p.MsoNormal
   {margin:0in;
   margin-bottom:.0001pt;
   text-indent:.2in;
   font-size:10.0pt;}
```

If you see this value, change it to 0 (zero):

```
p.MsoNormal
   {margin:0in;
   margin-bottom:0;
   text-indent:.2in;
   font-size:10.0pt;}
```

Repeat wherever you find `margin-bottom:.0001pt`.

Change 0in (or 0cm) Values to 0

Wherever you see a margin value of 0in (or 0cm if you used metric measurements), change to 0:

```
p.MsoNormal
   {margin:0;
   margin-bottom:0;
   text-indent:.2in;
   font-size:10.0pt;}
```

Change Left/Right Margins and Text Indents to Percentages

Next you need to change any right- or left-margin indents, and any text indents, from inches to percentages. A text-indent refers to the first line of text (a first-line indent); a margin refers to the indentation of a whole paragraph.

The reason we use percentages in left/right margins and first-line indents is to ensure the margins remain constant no matter the size of font the user selects to read your ebook in. If you use ems, then as the user increases their screen font size the margin will also increase and can create a display issue.

For a first-line indent I find that between 3% and 5% displays nicely. In this case I change my `text-indent:.2in` to `text-indent:3%`:

```
p.MsoNormal
  {margin:0;
  margin-bottom:0;
  text-indent:3%;
  font-size:10.0pt;}
```

If you created any hanging paragraphs, you will have both a margin-left value and a negative text-indent value to change. For example:

```
p.Hanging1
  {margin-top:0;
  margin-right:0;
  margin-bottom:12.0pt;
  margin-left:3%;
  text-indent:-3%;
  font-size:10.0pt;}
```

For cascading (multilevel) indents, I start with a first-level indent of 3% (to match the first-line indent of the main paragraphs), then increase by 3% for each level. Be mindful that if you use both left- and right-margin indents, the right margin should be the same for every level; only the left-margin indent increases.

Change Top/Bottom Margins to Ems

For top and bottom margins you need to use ems instead of percentages. This ensures the line spacing remains consistent with the font size as the user changes it. If you want a single line space, use 1em. A double space would be 2em, and so on. A half-inch (36pt in Word) is about 3em:

```
p.MsoTitle
  {margin-top:3em;
  margin-right:0;
  margin-bottom:3em;
  margin-left:0;
  text-align:center;
  font-size:20.0pt;}
```

For values below 10pt, use decimals: 6pt becomes .6em, for example.

Change Point Values to Ems

Now change all remaining point values to em values. Using the system of 10pt = 1em, change your body text to 1em:

```
p.MsoNormal
   {margin:0;
   margin-bottom:0;
   text-indent:3%;
   font-size:1em;}
```

For all others, change accordingly. For example, `h1` becomes:

```
h1
   {margin-top:2.4em;
   margin-right:0;
   margin-bottom:2.4em;
   margin-left:0;
   text-align:center;
   font-size:1.8em;
   font-weight:bold;}
```

Again, for values below 10pt, use decimals.

Avoid Automatic First-Line Indent

All Kindle ereaders and apps, as well as some ePub devices and apps, have an irritating default whereby they will automatically indent the first line of every paragraph if no first-line indent is defined in the code. This is a pain if you wish to have paragraphs or headings flushed left (like in this manual).

The problem arises because Word does not include a text-indent attribute in a style definition if you do not use a first-line indent. In the example below I created a style called First that flushed left the first paragraph of each chapter. But Word has not put in a text-indent value in the style definition:

```
p.First
   {margin:0;
   margin-bottom:0;
   font-size:1em;}
```

In order to prevent the automatic first-line indent, **you need to add a text-indent attribute with a value of zero to all paragraph styles that do not contain a text-indent attribute:**

```
p.First
  {margin:0;
  margin-bottom:0;
  text-indent:0;
  font-size:1em;}
```

This is true even for text that is centered. If you do not add the attribute, then the first line of any centered text will be indented, creating off-center text.

Justify Text Alignment (optional)

All Amazon ereaders and apps will automatically justify text to mimic the block look of print books. However, in some Kindle devices the user has the option to turn off auto-justification in favour of a jagged right margin.

If the code in your ebook forces justification, this will override the user's option to turn off justification in their ereader. According to Amazon, this results in "poor reader experience." (So why Amazon do not allow the reader to turn off auto-justification in *all* Kindle devices and apps is a mystery.) To assuage these readers, you must *not* put in any kind of forced justification in your CSS.

ePub device and app manufacturers are also inconsistent. For example, my Kobo Touch allows the user to choose whether or not to justify text, but my Aldiko for Android app only does if the user turns off *all* publisher formatting. Apple's iBooks reader auto-justifies text but the user can turn this off.

Critics of auto-justification point to the poor job that many ereaders make of word spacing, and over the years device manufacturers have vacillated between hyphenating to fix the problem, then not hyphenating, and back again. Amazon now claim to have solved the problem with their Enhanced Typesetting; the jury is still out.

So what do you do? Do you leave your CSS as is and let the user decide but risk annoying those with devices or apps that do not justify the text? Or do you force justify and risk annoying those who hate the rivers of white space created by poor justification and who cannot turn it off due to your code?

In the past I favoured forced justification because I wanted to ensure my ebook mimicked the look of a print book. I have never had a reader complain. Nevertheless, I have since changed my position because my own reading experience on digital devices has shown me that I don't really find a jagged right margin as off-putting as I once thought. So I now leave the option open to the user where such an option exists. If it doesn't, and the device or app does not force justify, well, so be it.

That said, if there are circumstances where justification is absolutely essential to you as the publisher, you can add a `text-align:justify` attribute/value to any style where it is desired. For example:

```
p.MsoNormal
   {margin:0;
   margin-bottom:0;
   text-indent:3%;
   text-align:justify;
   font-size:1em;}
```

Avoid Auto-Justification (optional)

There are instances where a device's auto-justification looks horrible and you need to override this. My experience is that headings intended to flush left look very unsightly if they are force justified by the ereader. Lengthy website addresses look even worse. Poetry is destroyed. Bullets and hanging paragraphs are pulled out of alignment.

In any style where you need to avoid auto-justification, you must add a `text-align:left` attribute/value. For example:

```
h2
   {margin-top:0;
   margin-right:0;
   margin-bottom:1em;
   margin-left:0;
   text-indent:0;
   text-align:left;
   font-size:1.5em;
   font-weight:bold;}
```

However, some devices and apps will ignore the left value and justify anyway. My experience is that Kindle devices and apps do not, and my Kobo Touch also does not. I've heard mixed reviews of Apple devices and apps. One can only code as one can; how device manufacturers program is beyond our control.

Avoid Overlapping Text (optional)

Amazon and others will warn you not to add any fixed line-height attributes as this will interfere with the user's ability to adjust line height to suit their reading preferences. While this works well when text is sized 1em or less, larger text can overlap if the screen size forces a line of text to run over to the next line.

The problem occurs with some ePub readers and apps but not Kindle, is more common with cellphones or small-screen ereaders, and more likely to occur if the user increases their font size to aid in legibility.

The solution is to set a line-height attribute with a value of no less than 120%:

```
h1
   {margin-top:2.4em;
   margin-right:0;
   margin-bottom:2.4em;
   margin-left:0;
   text-align:center;
   text-indent:0;
   font-size:1.8em;
   line-height:120%;
   font-weight:bold;}
```

If the user sets the line height in their ereader to 1.5 (150%) or double (200%), this 120% will override the user's preference; however, because you are limiting this code to your headings and title page text, the effect is less noticeable and annoying.

Check Your CSS

Click on your document tab and look at it in Book View. Does anything look awry? I immediately notice that my subtitle is off-center; when I check the CSS I see a `text-indent:3%` there. That was the result of my having forgotten to remove the first-line indent in that style. I change the value from 3% to 0 to fix.

I also feel there is too much space before and after my title (imagine it on a screen as small as a smartphone). So I reduce my top and bottom margins from 3em to 2em. This looks better so I leave these at 2em.

You can tinker with the values as necessary to achieve the best look for your ebook. Just remember to be consistent.

Validate Your CSS (optional)

Once you feel everything looks good, you have the option to validate your CSS online using a handy Sigil tool; note that you must be connected to the Internet to do so.

From the toolbar select Tools > Validate Stylesheets with W3C. Sigil will open your default browser, connect to the W3C CSS Validation website, and automatically upload your CSS. If no problems are found, you will get a "Congratulations! No Error Found" message. If errors are found, the website will return details of the error(s) and a list of which parts of your CSS are valid. If you break your CSS right at the first entry, you will be told no valid CSS was found.

For example, for the purpose of illustration I deliberately deleted the closing bracket on my `h1` style. W3C returned the error, noting it happened in the `h1` style, creating a parsing error for `MsoTitle`, which follows `h1` (which is why W3C calls this two errors, not one). Below the error you will see that the only valid CSS is p.`MsoNormal`, because the first entry after that is where I broke my CSS (Fig. 2.9).

NOTE: Whether you place the opening bracket on the same line as the style name (as W3C does) or at the opening of the style's attributes (as Word does and which I have replicated in this manual) is irrelevant. Similarly, whether you place the closing bracket on its own line or at the end of the last value is also irrelevant.

If you error within a style, W3C will return the error and tell you how to fix it. To illustrate, I deleted the semicolon of the `margin-bottom: 0;` value in p.`MsoNormal` (Fig. 2.10). W3C returns the error that the semicolon is missing.

Step 5: Clean Out Your Document

Word (and other word processors) has a habit of leaving behind bits of stray code that can cause havoc in your ebook. In every manuscript I have converted for myself and others I have found code that needed to be cleaned out: inexplicable language changes; hidden text color changes; stray code left behind by deleted text boxes, table of contents, or lists; misplaced Italic and Bold text; and so on.

If one uses an auto-convertor to build an ebook, the convertor doesn't remove this stray code; instead, it creates a new style class to accommodate

Fig. 2.9

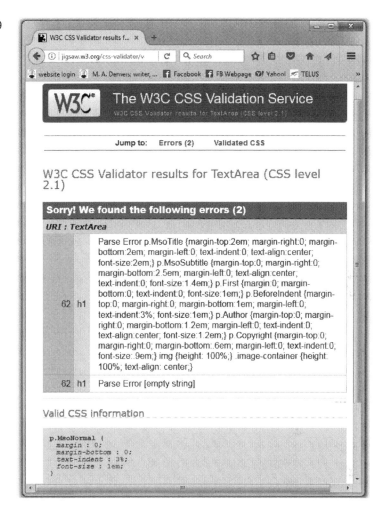

the code and adds the new style to your CSS. This is exactly what you do *not* want and which is why using auto-convertors is so problematic.

Luckily, however, you are using Sigil and can find and remove this wayward code. Better still, such errors are easy to find for two reasons: 1) all code is colored in Sigil, so it stands out against the black text; and 2) the code you'll be seeking has specific characteristics that you can quickly scan for using Sigil's Find module.

Body Language and WordSection1 Element

At the top of your document, below `</head>`, you will see something like this:

```
<body lang="EN-US" style='text-justify-
trim:punctuation'>
<div class="WordSection1">
```

The first line is the body language code we discussed last chapter, and will vary depending on which editing language you chose. The body language attribute may or may not contain a style, but the one shown here, `'text-justify-trim:punctuation'`, is one I have not seen before and is indicative of the kind of weird stuff that Word can spit out and which will often cause your ePub to fail validation. The second line is a division

Fig. 2.10

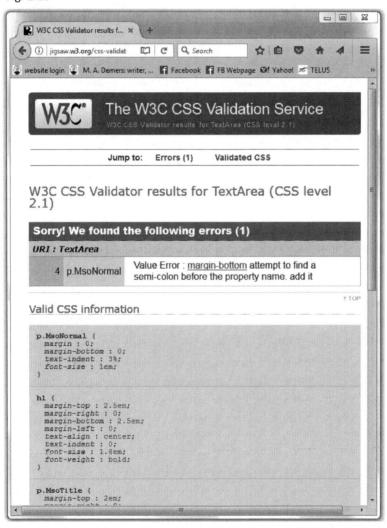

class that Word creates in case you use more than one section in your document. **Delete all attributes in your body tag so you are left only with:**

    <body>

Delete the second line of code, `<div class="WordSection1">`. Then scroll down to the very bottom of your document where you will find:

    </div>
    </body>
    </html>

Delete ONLY `</div>`.

Inline Styling

Inline styling refers to modifications made solely in the HTML and which do not link back to the CSS. Most inline styling starts with the `<span>` tag and closes with its corresponding `</span>` tag. The text that falls between the opening and closing tags is the text affected by the styling. For example, in

    <p class="MsoNormal">As William said,<span
    style='color:#131313'>"There are more things in
    Heaven and Earth, Horatio, than are dreamt of in
    your philosophy."</span></p>

the inline styling is a color change and affects "'There are more things in Heaven and Earth, Horatio, than are dreamt of in your philosophy.'"

This example is typical of text likely taken off the Internet. Here the author has found the quote he wanted then copied and pasted it off the Net without first scrubbing the text. The result is that he inadvertently brought in code that colors the text. The color #131313 is 93% Black, which is why the author never noticed the change in the text color. This code, however, will cause problems if the user changes their device from Day Mode (black text on white background) to Night Mode (white text on black background): the 93% Black text will not change to white; it will disappear into the black background. Consequently, the inline styling must be deleted:

    <p class="MsoNormal">As William said,"There are
    more things in Heaven and Earth, Horatio, than are
    dreamt of in your philosophy."</p>

Another common example is a font size change:

```
<p class="MsoNormal">"Welcome, welcome," <span
style='font-size:9.0pt'>he greeted us with a heavy
French accent.</span></p>
```

Here, the font size change was only one point difference from the main text and as such the author never noticed it. But that fixed size of 9pt will cause the styled text to remain 9pt regardless of the font size set by the user, and must be removed:

```
<p class=MsoNormal>"Welcome, welcome," he greeted
us with a heavy French accent.</p>
```

There is an abundance of possible examples I could show you of unwanted code lurking in Word documents. You don't have to know why or how it came to be there, you just need to remove it.

To find such wayward code, I simply use Sigil's Find module. Type in

```
<span
```

then check each one you find. If you find any inline styling that is not supposed to be there, remove it.

You may ask, How do I know if it's not supposed to be there? The answer is, Did you deliberately put it there? For example, say you applied a French-language style to a selection of text:

```
<p class="MsoNormal"><span lang=FR>"S'il vous
plaît, Monsieur."</span></p>
```

This is correct: you put it there and it is required. So you would leave that in. However, let's say you later edited the text to remove the French but forgot to take out the language styling:

```
<p class="MsoNormal"><span lang=FR>"If you please,
sir," he said with a heavy French accent.</span></
p>
```

By failing to delete the language styling, you inadvertently coded a whole paragraph of English as French. This will cause the wrong dictionary to open if the reader uses their device's built-in dictionaries to look up the meaning of a word in that paragraph. You need to remove the language styling:

```
<p class="MsoNormal">"If you please, sir," he said
with a heavy French accent.</p>
```

TIP: You can search either up or down through your manuscript. At the bottom of the Sigil window, below the Replace field, there is a Mode button whose default option is Down. You can change to Up as needed.

P Tag Inline Styling

Another form of wayward code is inline styling hidden in the paragraph (`<p>`) tag. For example:

```
<p class="MsoNormal" style='text-indent:.5in'>She bought pizza for dinner.</p>
```

This was caused by a tab left behind at the start of a paragraph, and must be removed:

```
<p class="MsoNormal">She bought pizza for dinner.</p>
```

To find such inline style changes, search for

```
style=
```

If you have properly created styles for all your formatting needs, you will not see any inline styling in the paragraph tag.

Often such inline styling is the result of the author failing to apply the appropriate style. For example, what should have been Heading 1 was left as Normal and centered:

```
<p class="MsoNormal" align=center style='text-align:center'>Chapter One</p>
```

To fix this, simply change the opening and closing tags to Heading 1:

```
<h1>Chapter One</h1>
```

If you do find inline styling that needs to be there, create a new style that achieves the same effect and use that instead. See "Creating New Style Classes" in "Advanced Formatting."

Abandoned Anchors

An anchor is a target of a hyperlink. Anchors are created automatically by Word if you use its automated Table of Contents module. If you later delete this table of contents, Word still leaves the anchors behind:

```
<h1><a name="_Toc466994272">Chapter One</a></h1>
```

These anchors should be removed:

```
<h1>Chapter One</h1>
```

Similarly, if you created internal links but later removed the hyperlinked text, the anchor you linked to will still be lurking in your manuscript.

The fastest way to find anchors is to do a search for

```
name=
```

then remove any abandoned anchors and their closing tags (`</a>`).

Reformat Anchors

If you have any hyperlinked text (such as footnotes) that you need to keep in your manuscript, the code `name=` must be changed. This is because the attribute `name=` is not used in XHTML and will cause your ePub to fail validation. To fix this, change `name` to `id` in all such hyperlinks:

```
<a href="#_ftn8" name="_ftnref8" title=""><span
 class="MsoFootnoteReference">[8]</span></a>
```

becomes

```
<a href="#_ftn8" id="_ftnref8" title=""><span
class="MsoFootnoteReference>[8]</span></a>
```

Create a Section for Your Footnotes

If you have footnotes in your manuscript, when Word exports to HTML it converts all footnotes to endnotes and places a page break and a thin black line in the document just above the endnotes. The code will look something like this:

```
<br clear="all" />
<hr align=left size=1 width="33%" />
```

XHTML will not recognize any of this, so **delete it.** In its place, create a Heading 1 called Endnotes:

```
<h1>Endnotes</h1>
```

This serves two purposes: 1) it provides an obvious heading entry for your endnotes; and 2) it can later be added to your table of contents. When you later split your document into chapters/sections, Endnotes will be a new one.

Remove Inserted Page Breaks

This only applies if you created any page breaks using the Insert > Page Break method in Word and forgot to delete them. If you did, in your document you will find:

```
<br clear="all" style='page-break-before:always'>
```

This code will cause your ePub to fail validation and must be deleted. The page breaks you need will be added later.

Forgotten Formatting

One final bit of wayward code is forgotten Italic or Bold (and Emphasis and Strong if you used them). This is almost always the result of formatting not just the text but the surrounding blank space, then later editing the text to remove the formatting but failing to include the blank space. In doing so you don't realize you've left behind stray code. For example:

```
<p class="MsoNormal">I italicized a<i> </i>word
then changed my mind.</p>
```

You can see how there is no text between the Italic tags, only the blank space; consequently, when you looked at your manuscript in Word nothing appeared awry. But that hidden code can cause odd text behaviour in some ereaders.

Again, you can use Sigil's Find module to seek out any stray Italic (`<i>`) or Bold (`<b>`). If you used Emphasis (`<em>`) or Strong (`<strong>`) in your document, look for those too. Remember to remove both the opening and closing tags, and to type the space back in:

```
<p class="MsoNormal">I italicized a word then
changed my mind.</p>
```

TIP: In Find, you can perform these tasks more efficiently by performing a Regex search. To find all wayward Italic elements, for example, in the Find field type in:

```
<i> *</i>
```

(Note the space before the asterisk. This is important!) Below the Find field are three Mode buttons; change the default Normal button to Regex. Click on Find. What Sigil will now find is any instance of an empty Italic element that contains zero spaces to any number of spaces.

Fix Miscellaneous Errors

Check your manuscript in Book View. Does any of the text look awry? If so, click on the incorrect paragraph and then click back to Code View (or view them simultaneously with F10). Is your paragraph style incorrect? If not, change it to the correct style.

Did you forget to format a few words of text? If so, apply the formatting tags to it:

```
<i>italic</i>
<b>bold</b>
<em>italicized text to be emphasized by a TTS reader</em>
<strong>bold text to be emphasized by a TTS reader</strong>
<del>strikethrough</del>
```

Step 6: Create Your Links (optional)

Links are made up of two components, an anchor (the target) and a hyperlink (the text that points to the target). Links may be internal, pointing to other text or an image in your ebook, or links may be external, pointing to a webpage on the Internet.

Internal Links

To create an internal link, you must first create the anchor at the text or image you will be linking to. In this example I am linking "See CIP data" to the CIP data on the copyright page.

To create the anchor, in Code View I go to my copyright page and place my cursor at the start of the CIP data (line 31 in Fig. 2.11). I then click on the Anchor icon on the toolbar. A box will open with a field for the anchor name. I name it "CIP" and click OK (Fig. 2.11). Sigil adds the anchor, `<a id="CIP"></a>`, to the start of the line of code:

```
<a id="CIP"></a><p class="Copyright">Library and Archives Canada Cataloguing in Publication</p>
```

I then go to the text in my ebook and select "See CIP data" and click on the Link icon on the toolbar. A list of my book components (files, images, and any anchors) pops up. I select the anchor #CIP and click OK (Fig. 2.12). **NOTE:** Anchors are specified by the hashtag (#) symbol.

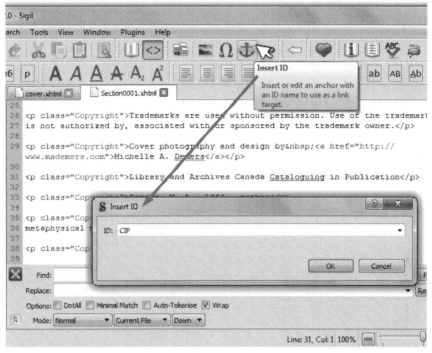
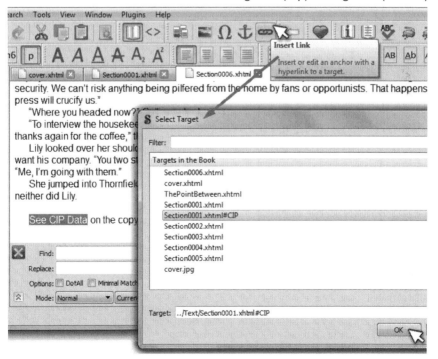

Fig. 2.11 (top) and Fig. 2.12 (bottom)

Sigil now hyperlinks the text to the anchor. In Code view I would see this:

```
<p class="MsoNormal"><a href="../Text/
ThePointBetween.xhtml#CIP">See CIP data</a> on the
copyright page for more information.</p>
```

Repeat as necessary for any links in your ebook.

WARNING: If linking to internal images, the process is the same: create an anchor then link to that anchor. Although all images appear in the list of components, do not link directly to an image; this will not work.

To test you links, simply click on the hyperlinked text and Sigil will jump to the anchor.

All ereaders and apps have a default method for displaying hyperlinked text. Most will turn the text blue and underline it, though others use a different color. How hyperlinked text is displayed is a function of the device's programming, not your CSS.

External Links

To create an external link, select the text you want hyperlinked then click on the Link icon. In the window that opens type in the website address including the "http" preface. Click OK. Your hyperlinked text is now created.

To test, click on the hyperlink. Sigil will open your default browser to the web location.

WARNING: Most retailers will not allow links to competitor sites, subscriber sign-up forms, or affiliate sites.

NOTE: When you split your document (next step), Sigil automatically updates your links to point to the correct file. You can add links at any stage in the ebook process, but creating them before you split your document is simply easier because you don't have to jump between text files.

Step 7: Create Your "Page" Breaks

When an ereader encounters a new XHTML file, the ereader automatically displays it on a fresh screen. This mimics the page breaks you find in print books. The next step, then, is to break your document up into multiple XHTML files.

Place your cursor at the end of the last line of text of the first section of your document (in most books this will be the end of your title page). This is most easily done in Book View. Then hit Ctrl+Enter.

A new file, Section001.xhtml, that contains all your remaining document text (Fig. 2.13) will appear and open. In the Book Browser pane you will see this new file under Text and directly below your initial book file. If you click back on this initial XHTML file, it now contains only your title page text.

Scroll down to the end of your next section (likely your copyright page). Hit Ctrl+Enter. Section002.xhtml is created and Section001.xhtml now contains only your copyright text.

Continue on down through your document, creating a new XHTML file wherever you want a break.

TIP: If you make a mistake, simply right-click on the XHTML file you created and select Merge. This will merge it back into the previous file and you can create your break again.

The order of the XHTML files determines the order the ereader displays them. **Do not change this order unless you need to change the order of your chapters or other sections.** If you do need to change the order, simply drag and drop the XHTML file to wherever in the order you want it to be.

Fig. 2.13

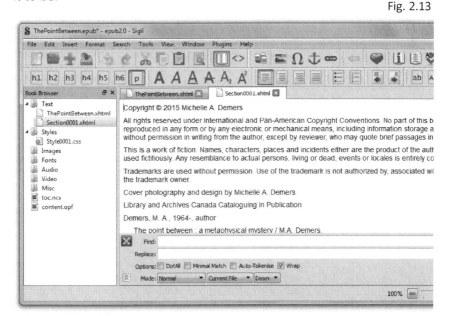

Step 8: Add Your Cover

All retailers require your cover be portrait style, in the sRGB color space, saved at 300 ppi to 350 ppi, and in the JPEG or PNG formats only.

If you need to make only one ePub file to sell across all retailers (except Amazon), I would use the Kindle image size. This way you do not have to make two different covers, one for Kindle and one for ePub.

Kindle books and ePubs require the cover to be embedded in the ebook file, but they do so in different ways. This section will address ePub code; Kindle cover code will be dealt with in the next chapter, "Convert to Kindle."

Size Requirements

Amazon recommend a marketing cover image of no less than 2700 pixels on the long side and no less than 1688 pixels in width, and no more than 5MB in size. (The Kindle Direct Publishing website says 50MB, but *Amazon Kindle Publishing Guidelines* says 5MB.) This file is uploaded separately when you upload your ebook.

In the early days of KDP, one did not embed the cover in your ebook; your marketing cover was copied and added to the ebook by Amazon during the ingestion process. *Amazon Kindle Publishing Guidelines* now states that a cover must be embedded in the file, but only that you need to use "a large, high-resolution" image and if it is too small it will be rejected. Most publishers simply use the same image file size as the marketing cover.

For Apple, Kobo, and B&N's Nook, your cover image is also your marketing image. Your cover is embedded in your ebook and, if you contract directly with any of these retailers, also uploaded separately as your marketing image when you upload your files to your account.

For **Apple**, your embedded cover must be a minimum of 1400 pixels on the short side (width), but no larger than 4,000,000 pixels total. To determine your pixel count, multiply the length and width. For example, if your cover is 2000 pixels by 1500 pixels, the total is 3,000,000 pixels. There is no size limit to the marketing cover image.

Kobo recommend a cover image no larger than 3MB. Average dimensions are 800 x 1224 pixels, but that's really too small for their high-resolution devices. I usually use the same cover as I use for Kindle; if you want to use something smaller, aim for at least 1800 pixels on the long side as this is the screen height of Kobo's latest device.

B&N's Nook require cover images of no less than 750 pixels in width but prefer no less than 1400 pixels in width to accommodate high-resolution devices.

Upload Your Cover File Into Sigil

In the Book Browser window, right-click on the Images folder and select Add Existing Files... Navigate to the folder on your computer where you have stored your cover image. Add it to the folder.

If you have named your cover image anything other than cover.jpg (or cover.png), rename it in Sigil or rename it before adding it into Sigil.

Specify Your Cover Image

In the Images folder, right-click on your cover image and select Cover Image. A check mark will now appear beside this.

Add Cover

You have two options for adding your cover, Sigil's handy one-click Add Cover module, or the more convoluted Apple option.

Sigil's Add Cover module creates a cover file and places it at the top of your Text folder, and places your cover image in an SVG wrapper. The SVG wrapper is a tried-and-true method of ensuring your cover looks correct on most ePub devices and apps. This is by far the easiest way to create your cover: on the toolbar select Tools > Add Cover.

However, the SVG wrapper is banned by Apple because of a problem with their iBooks reader whereby images often split over two screens; rather than fix the problem, or to program their devices to work with the SVG wrapper, Apple demand that images be placed in containers as a workaround. The use of containers to prevent image splitting is cumbersome and convoluted.

Unfortunately, Google Play tend to follow Apple's lead. In older Kobo devices the SVG wrapper works, but new devices seem to be programmed to ignore it; Kobo now state they prefer that image size be controlled in the CSS (though this may have more to do with selling to Mac users and less to do with real Kobo technological needs).

So if you need to create only one ePub file for use across all ePub platforms, you have no choice but to accommodate Apple. This code works on other platforms but it will later interfere with adding internal images to your ebook, if that is your intention.

If you also have internal images, read the sections "Frames" and "Internal Images," both in "Advanced Formatting." Then decide which way you want to go with your cover.

Apple Method Step 1: Add CSS Class

To accommodate Apple, you need to create a class to control the image size, and another class for the division container for your cover image; together they force the image to fit on the screen. Open your Style0001.css. Scroll down to the bottom and add (Fig 2.14):

```
img
  {height:100%;}
.image-container
  {height:100%;
  text-align:center;}
```

Fig. 2.14

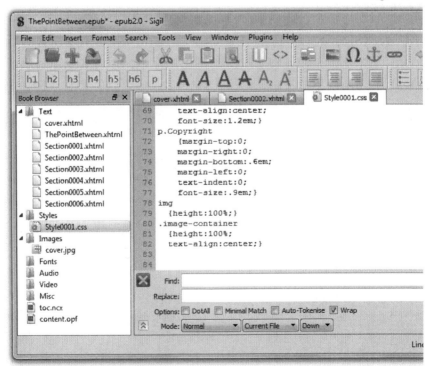

Step 2: Create a New XHTML File

In Code View, under Book Browser, right-click on the Text folder and select Add Blank HTML File. This will create a new XHTML file at the bottom of your Text folder. Drag and drop this new file to the top of the list under Text. Then right-click on it and select Rename. Rename the file cover.xhtml.

Right-click on the file and select Link Stylesheets... Select "Style001.css" and click OK.

Step 3: Insert Your Cover

Click on your cover.xhtml file tab. In Code View, just below `<body>`, add:

```
<div class="image-container">
```

Hit Enter, then click on the picture icon on the toolbar OR select Insert > File. From the Insert File box select your cover image and click OK (Fig. 2.15). Hit Enter again and type in:

```
</div>
```

If done correctly, the whole of your cover file code will look like this:

```
<?xml version="1.0" encoding="utf-8"?>
<!DOCTYPE html PUBLIC "-//W3C//DTD XHTML 1.1//EN"
   "http://www.w3.org/TR/xhtml11/DTD/xhtml11.dtd">
<html xmlns="http://www.w3.org/1999/xhtml">
<head>
<title></title>
<link href="../Styles/Style0001.css" type="text/css" rel="stylesheet"/>
</head>
<body>
<div class="image-container">
<img alt="cover" src="../Images/cover.jpg"/>
</div>
</body>
</html>
```

Your cover will now appear in the Sigil window, shrunk to fit. If you resize the window you will see that the cover image resizes accordingly.

TIP: You can skip steps 2 and 3 of the Apple method by using Sigil's Add Cover module then replacing everything between `<body>` and `</body>` in the cover.xhtml file with:

Fig. 2.15

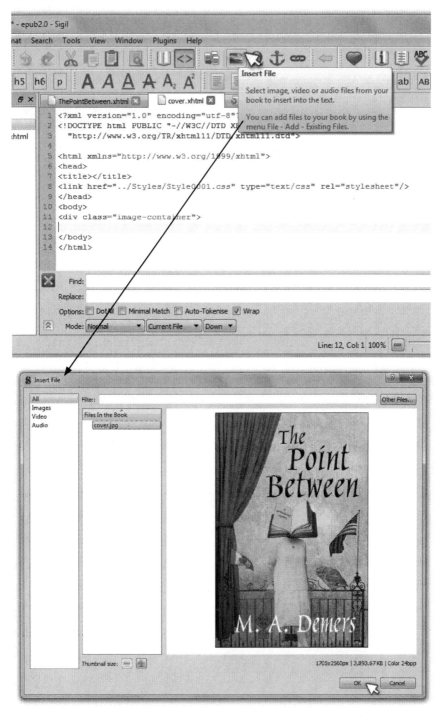

```
<div class="image-container">
<img alt="cover" src="../Images/cover.jpg"/>
</div>
```

Add Backup HTML (optional)

Placing your cover in a division container works great—until, that is, your reader turns off publisher formatting. Then your cover balloons up to its full pixel dimensions, which may or may not fit on the screen. The way to avoid this is to add backup inline styling. This styling is redundant if the CSS remains connected but does not create any display issues, and will ensure your cover fits on the screen, and is centered on the screen, if the CSS is disconnected by the user.

Place your cursor anywhere in:

```
<div class="image-container">
```

then click on the Center Paragraph icon on the Sigil toolbar or select Format > Center (Ctrl+E). This will change your code to:

```
<div class="image-container" style="text-align: center;">
```

Next, add a height attribute with a value of 100% to your `<img>` tag:

```
<img alt="cover" height="100%" src="../Images/cover.jpg"/>
```

Add Cover Description (optional)

Apple demand that your cover image contains a description which can be read to the visually impaired. In the code above, this is what is contained within the `alt=` attribute. Sigil by default puts the file name in, but Apple prefer something more descriptive. You can be as succinct or detailed as you want to be. This is my description for the cover of *The Point Between* placed in lieu of `"cover"`:

```
<img alt="The Point Between cover featuring a
woman in a white dress and whose head is an open
book on which is written A Metaphysical Mystery.
She is standing in front of iron gates on which
sits an owl and a sign that reads Dead End No
Beach Access. There is a red curtain and the
Canadian flag on the left, and an American flag on
the right. Behind her is the sky with faint pink
clouds." height="100%" src="../Images/cover.jpg">
```

Step 9: Build Your Table of Contents

All ebooks must have a table of contents, which you will now build automatically using Sigil's built-in TOC module. This module builds an NCX TOC, which does not exist as a file in the text folder of your ebook but as a separate file within the ebook archive. The NCX TOC is used not only to navigate the ebook but to add "page" markers that allow the ebook to be referenced properly in footnotes or a bibliography.

From the toolbar select View > Table of Contents (Alt+F3). Then select Tools > Table of Contents > Generate Table of Contents (Ctrl+T).

A new box will open that lists all text in your ebook that uses an `<h>` tag (Fig. 2.16). (*The Point Between* has no subheadings so I added some for illustrative purposes.)

You can see how the subheadings are cascaded in ascending order. Each heading is included by default; to exclude a heading, uncheck its box.

In the bottom-left corner is a button with "<Select headings to include in TOC>". In its drop-down menu are the options to: 1) include all headings;

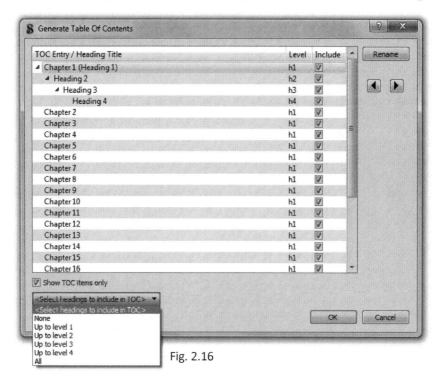

Fig. 2.16

2) include no headings at all; or 3) restrict your TOC to a specific heading level. Sigil will recognize up to six heading levels.

Once you have selected or deselected the appropriate headings, click OK. In the right of the Sigil window your table of contents now appears in the Table of Contents frame.

Edit Your Table of Contents (optional)

You can add any item to your table of contents that does not make use of an `<h>` tag. This is how you can add items such as your Cover, Title Page, Copyright Information, Acknowledgments, About the Author, Also By, and so on. **All ePubs should have, at the very least, an entry added for the cover.**

You can also rename your chapter headings. For example, you might have used only numbers in the actual headings but want to spell them out in the table of contents.

To make changes to your TOC, select Tools > Table of Contents > Edit Table of Contents. A box will open that lists everything currently in your TOC (Fig. 2.17).

To rename a TOC heading, simply double-click on the existing text, delete and rename as appropriate.

To add your cover entry, click on the first item in your TOC and then click on the Add Above button. A blank line will be added at the top of the list. Beneath TOC Entry/Heading Title double-click inside the blank line and type in "Cover" (no quotation marks). Then click on the Select Target button. Another box will open with all your XHTML files listed. Select "cover.xhtml".

Repeat in a similar fashion until you have added/renamed as many items in your TOC as necessary. When done, click on OK (Fig. 2.18).

NOTE: If you include subheadings in your TOC, Sigil automatically creates the anchors necessary to link to the TOC. You will then find in your target list not only the XHTML files but the anchors created by Sigil. Anchors are identified by a hashtag (#). All Sigil's default TOC anchors are prefaced with `#sigil_toc_id_` and added in numerical order. For example, the first subheading of chapter 1 will appear as:

```
Text/Section0002.xhtml#sigil_toc_id_1
```

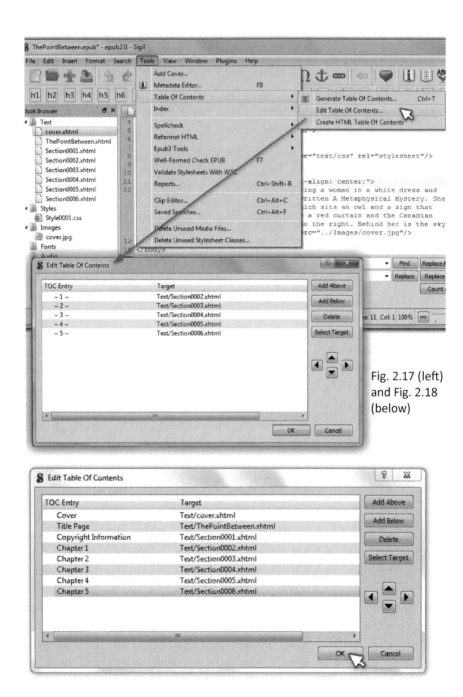

Fig. 2.17 (left) and Fig. 2.18 (below)

WARNING: No two entries in your TOC can point to the same target. If you need additional entries to point to the same file, you must create anchors within the file and point to those instead.

WARNING: The NCX TOC cannot contain entries that do not point to anchors. For example, many print books add section headings in the TOC but these section headings do not contain page numbers. Such additional information is not possible in an NCX TOC. If you want a custom TOC, you can add an HTML TOC that opens as a "page" in your book, the same as any other text. This is covered in the next chapter, "Convert to Kindle."

Step 10: Add Your Metadata

Metadata refers to information about your ebook's title, author, publisher, ISBN (if you have one), other contributors, and so on. Metadata is required in all ebooks, although only certain properties are mandatory.

To add your metadata, select Tools > Metadata Editor (F8). A box will open, MetaData Editor (Fig. 2.19). There will be two default values already entered, the version of Sigil used and the date you are working on the ebook. Beside the date will be a white arrow; if you click on it the details will appear, in this case the value is "modification".

Fig. 2.19

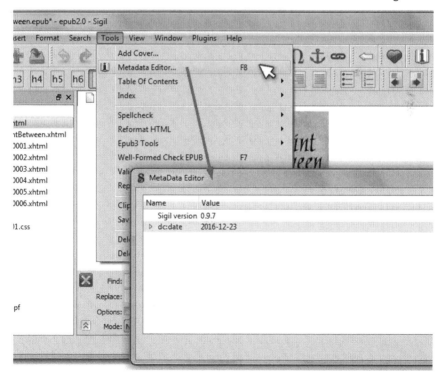

Fig. 2.20

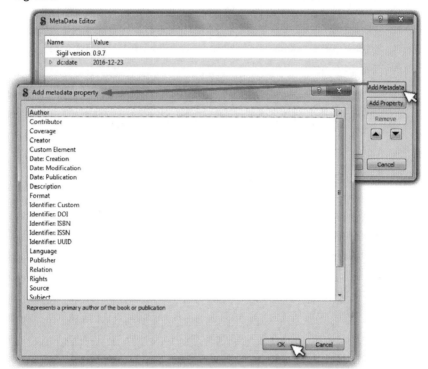

Click on the Add Metadata button. The Add Metadata Property box will open with a list of possible entries (Fig. 2.20).

It is mandatory to have at least one creator defined in the metadata. If you are the author of the ebook, in the Add Metadata Property box select Author and click OK. The box will close, and in the MetaData Editor box you will now see that the following entry has been added:

    dc:creator [No data]
      opf:role aut

Double-click on "[No data]" and type in your author name *exactly as it appears on your title page*.

If you share authorship of your book, you must repeat the above for every author credited on the title page.

If the book is a compilation for which you are the editor credited on the title page, in the Add Metadata Property box select Creator and click OK. With "dc:creator" still highlighted in the Edit MetaData box, click on Add Property. Select Role and choose "Editor of a compilation". Click OK. Replace [No data] with your name. You will then appear in retail catalogues correctly as "Your Name (Editor)" instead of "Your Name (Author)". Whether you input each author's name into the metadata is a contractual decision between you and the authors.

If there is anyone else credited on the title page—an illustrator, for example—**an entry for them in the metadata is also mandatory.** To add metadata for another contributor, select Creator and then choose the appropriate role.

The next mandatory property is Title. Click on Add Metadata. Scroll down the list to Title; select and click on OK. Replace the [No data] with the title of your book *exactly as it appears on your title page*.

The remaining mandatory properties are Publisher and **Language.** For Publisher, if you self-publishing under your own imprint put in the name of the imprint. If you do not have an imprint, put your own name in.

For Language, another box will open with a list of languages. Choose the appropriate one and Sigil will automatically add the property and value to the metadata.

If you are assigning an ISBN to your ebook, add this property but without the hyphens.

The date of publication is also mandatory, but at this point you may not have a firm date. When you upload your ebook to the retailer or aggregator, you will be asked then to input a date for publication; when you do, it will be added to your ebook's metadata by the retailer's or aggregator's ingestion system. Remember to be consistent across all retailers and/or aggregators.

All other metadata is optional.

Step 11: Validate Your ePub

The first step is to use Sigil's built-in validator, FlightCrew. FlightCrew is accessed by Tools > Well-Formed Check EPUB (F7).

If all is well, a Validation Results frame will open with a "No Problems Found!" message. If there are errors, each error's location and reason

Fig. 2.21 (top) and Fig. 2.22 (bottom)

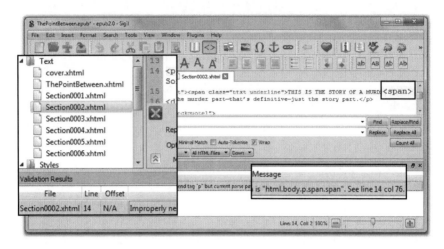

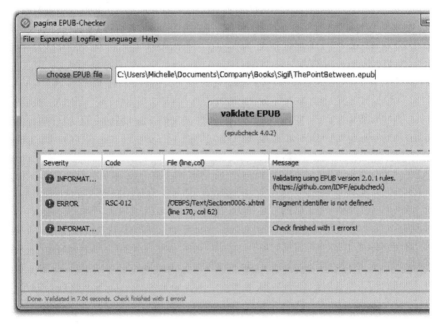

are listed (Fig. 2.21). To go to an error, double-click anywhere on the error's line. Sigil will open the file to the error location. In Fig. 2.21 I have forgotten to put the forward slash in the closing </span> tag.

NOTE: The location of an error is not always exact because forgetting to add the forward slash in an "empty element" (an element that does not require a corresponding closing tag, such as the line element (`<hr/>`) can fool Sigil into believing the problem lies farther down in the code where the next closing tag is found. But the clue to the real culprit will always be found in the error message.

If everything passes FlightCrew, the next step is to validate your ePub outside of Sigil. There are two reasons for this: 1) oftentimes different validators find different issues; and 2) retailers such as Kobo and Apple rely on the IDPF's official validator, EpubCheck, when processing your file. If it fails EpubCheck, your file will be rejected for distribution, so it is best to confirm the file passes before you upload.

To validate in EpubCheck, go to http://validator.idpf.org/. Here you will upload your ePub, and the IDPF's online validator will test your file and report back any issues. This of course requires an Internet connection, and your files must be smaller than 10MB.

If your files are larger than 10MB, or if you are not connected to the Internet, you can use **Pagina's ePUB-Checker**, which is built on the official open-source ePubCheck. I actually use ePUB-Checker even for those files smaller than 10MB simply because ePUB-Checker is quicker and I don't have to go online and upload my files. I only use the online validator as a final test for small files.

Install Pagina ePUB-Checker onto your desktop. Double-click on the Pagina icon to open the window. Drag and drop your ePub file into the open window. Click on Validate EPUB.

If there are errors, a list of them will appear along with where the error occurs. In this case I have a hyperlink for an anchor that was later deleted (Fig. 2.22).

As you can see, ePUB-Checker works exactly like FlightCrew: the error is listed along with its location. When you fix the error and recheck, your file will pass validation.

Step 12: Test Your ePub

The final step is to test the ePub in as many ePub apps and devices as possible. I always start with **Adobe Digital Editions** as this is the fastest. Only if it works here do I graduate to testing my file on physical devices and other apps.

Install Adobe Digital Editions. Associate ePubs files with ADE, or drag and drop your file onto the ADE icon on your desktop.

The file should automatically open to your cover (the first file in your ebook) (Fig. 2.23). Is your cover properly sized and centered on the screen?

To check your table of contents, click on the Show/Hide Navigation Panel icon on the toolbar. Your TOC will appear in a left frame (Fig. 2.24). Check each link in the TOC to make sure it is working correctly.

Fig. 2.23

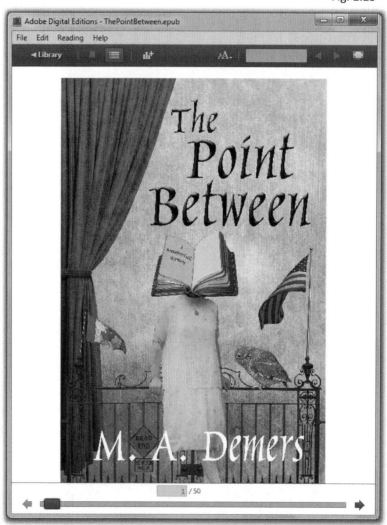

Build Your eBook • 77

Now work through your ebook screen by screen. As you do, check the following:

- Are all your paragraphs styled properly?
- Are there any line breaks you didn't deliberately put in?
- Are there any screen (section) breaks you didn't put in?
- Are you missing any section breaks?
- Do your internal links work?
- Do your external links work?

Fig. 2.24

If anything is incorrect, return to your file and fix your mistakes. If everything looks good, begin testing on devices and/or in apps.

When you close your file in ADE, you will be asked if you want to save it to your library. Click on Cancel to close your file without saving to the ADE library.

A Word About Publisher Formatting

Most ereaders offer the user the option to override select publisher formatting or to turn it off completely. Often users can change the line height and margin widths without affecting the rest of the ebook's formatting, and of course they can choose the font displayed. But if the user elects to turn off publisher formatting, this breaks the link between the ebook's content and the CSS.

If the link is broken, then your CSS is for naught. What happens then is that the ereader's default programming takes over. Body text and headings have default styles built into the ereader. For example, all `<p>` elements may be indented, while `<h1>` elements may be enlarged, bolded, and centered. Screen breaks are added before any `<h1>` element, and in some ereaders also before `<h2>` elements. And so on.

If the CSS link is broken, inline styling such as Italic or Emphasis will display because it is not dependent on the CSS. However, any CSS class applied to inline styling will not display.

If your ebook makes use of complex formatting, it is recommended that you warn your readers up front not to turn off publisher formatting.

3 Convert to Kindle

To convert your ePub to Kindle requires only a few modifications to your file. **Create a copy to work on so you do not overwrite your ePub.** I usually create a file with "_Kindle" added to the file name to differentiate my ePub from my Kindle ePub file.

Step 1: Delete Cover File

Kindle handles cover images differently, so begin by deleting cover.xhtml from your Text folder: right-click on the file, then choose Delete.

In the Images folder, right-click on your cover image file and uncheck Cover Image.

Step 2: Specify Cover

Open the Content.opf file (Fig. 3.1). Scroll down until you see:

    <manifest>

Fig. 3.1

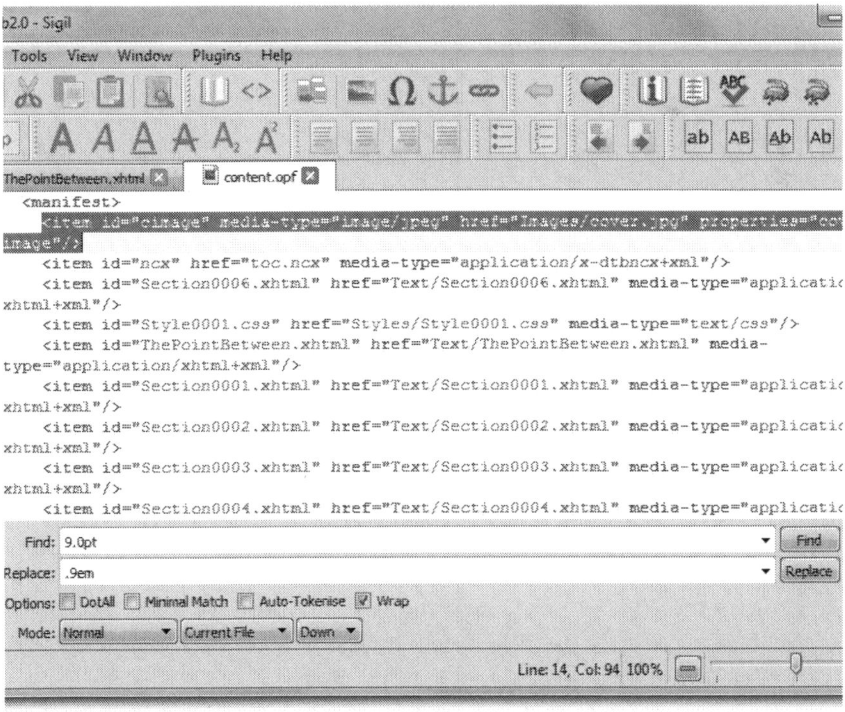

Just beneath this, add the following line of code (no line break):

```
<item id="cimage" media-type="image/jpeg"
href="Images/cover.jpg" properties="cover-image"/>
```

Step 3: Remove Apple Cover Code

If you chose the Apple cover option, delete from your CSS:

```
img
  {height:100%;}
.image-container
  {height:100%;
   text-align:center;}
```

Step 4: Edit TOC

In your Table of Contents, delete the entry for the cover.

Step 5: Add the HTML Table of Contents

Kindle books require two TOCs, the NCX TOC we already created and which is particular to ePubs, and an HTML TOC that is a legacy of early Kindle books that did not make use of an NCX TOC.

When the user clicks on the Table of Contents option from their Kindle Go To menu, it links to the HTML TOC. To access the NCX TOC, the user must click on a separate Table of Contents link, usually found in another, collapsible panel. Older-model Kindles do not have this option, which is why all Kindle books still require an HTML TOC.

Sigil has a handy module whereby it will create an HTML copy of your NCX TOC. Select Tools > Table of Contents > Create HTML Table of Contents (Fig. 3.2).

Sigil then places this TOC in an XHTML file at the start of your ebook. It also creates a second CSS, sgc.toc.css, to define the styles of the TOC (Fig. 3.3), and adds the reference in the guide section of the Content.opf.

Amazon prefer that the TOC follow the natural order of a print book; that is, that the TOC follow the title page, copyright page, and any other front matter such as Acknowledgements. Drag and drop the TOC.xhtml to the

Convert to Kindle • 81

Fig. 3.2 (top) and Fig. 3.3 (bottom)

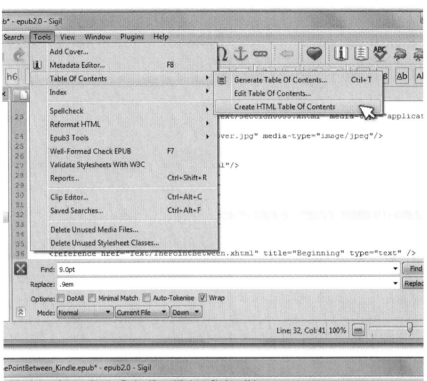

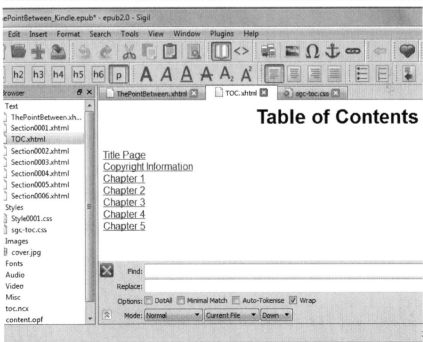

appropriate spot in your Text folder lineup. In my case I place it after my copyright page, which is my second file (Fig. 3.3).

You can leave the HTML TOC as is or you can change it to suit. I personally prefer my title to read only "Contents" so I edit out "Table of". I also prefer the title to be flushed left, so I open the sgc.toc.css and change the default CSS from

```
div.sgc-toc-title {
    font-size: 2em;
    font-weight: bold;
    margin-bottom: 1em;
    text-align: center;}
```

to

```
div.sgc-toc-title {
    font-size: 2em;
    font-weight: bold;
    margin-bottom: 1em;
    text-align: left;}
```

Because this new TOC is an HTML file, it can also be edited to add text which does not point to anywhere in your ebook. For example, you can add sections and line breaks between them. Editing the HTML TOC is covered in "Advanced Formatting."

NOTE: You may notice that Sigil puts a space between the attribute's colon and the value, while Word does not. This makes no difference in HTML.

Step 6: Add Start Reference

Kindle books require a guide item that indicates where you want your Kindle book to open when first opened by the consumer. This is usually the title page or the first chapter, but it does not have to be; however, you cannot link to the cover image. (This is allegedly because research data indicates users prefer to start reading right away rather than having to scroll forward from the cover.)

In this example we will open on the title page. Open your title page file. In Code View, at the beginning of the first line of text, insert an anchor and call it "Start" (no quotation marks, those are added by Sigil):

```
<a id="Start"></a><p class="MsoTitle">The Point Between</p>
```

In the Content.opf file, scroll down to:

```
<guide>
```

Just below it, add (no line break):

```
<reference href="Text/[file name].xhtml#Start"
title="Beginning" type="text" />
```

whereby [file name] is the name of the title page file where you placed the anchor in. In my example, the file is ThePointBetween.xhtml:

```
<reference href="Text/ThePointBetween.xhtml#Start"
title="Beginning" type="text" />
```

Although the above is historically how Amazon have directed the guide item to be created, technically speaking the Start anchor is no longer necessary. All that is necessary is the appropriate guide item in the Content.opf that specifies the file to be opened:

```
<reference href="Text/ThePointBetween.xhtml"
title="Beginning" type="text" />
```

However, when you test this in Kindle Previewer the ebook will open to the cover instead of the start file. This is a quirk of Previewer and does not indicate the actual behaviour of a Kindle device or app.

If you do not provide your own Start guide item, Amazon add one during the ingestion process. Critics have complained Amazon sometimes change the publisher-defined location of the Start tag, though I cannot confirm this.

Step 7: Update Metadata

If you are using separate ISBNs for your ePub and Kindle formats (you should but not everyone does), then you must update the metadata to change the ISBN from the ePub one to the Kindle one.

Step 8: Convert to Mobi File

Download and install **Kindle Previewer (2.94)** and **Kindle Previewer3**. Drag and drop your Kindle ePub file onto the Kindle Previewer icon on your desktop. This activates Kindlegen, the convertor that will change your ePub file into a mobi file. The Kindle Previewer window will open along with a message telling you your ebook is being compiled.

If all goes well, you will get a message that the compilation was successful (Fig. 3.4). If you then click on OK, the ebook will open in the Kindle Previewer window to the start position.

If there are any issues, you will either get a failure to compile warning, or a successful compilation but with warnings. If the latter, click on the arrow across from "Compilation Details" and scroll down until you find the problem(s). For the purpose of illustration I left out the Text part of the href target:

```
<reference href="ThePointBetween.xhtml"
title="Beginning" type="text" />
```

Fig. 3.4

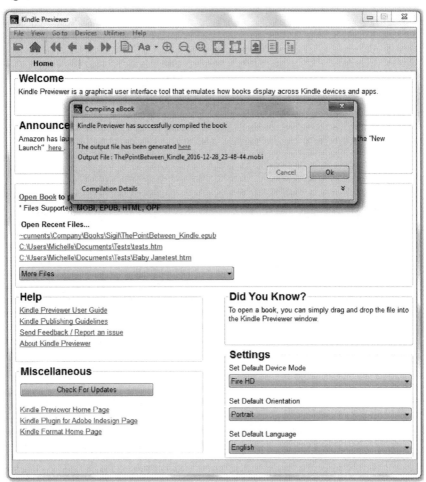

This returned the following three errors in Kindlegen (Fig. 3.5):

> Warning(prcgen):W14001: Hyperlink not resolved: C:\Users\Michelle\AppData\Local\Temp\mbp_7E1_1_4_B_2F_2A_113_10FC_17A0_1\OEBPS\ThePointBetween.xhtml
>
> Warning(prcgen):W14002: Some hyperlinks could not be resolved.
>
> Warning(prcgen):W14003: The start reading location could not be resolved.

If you see more then one error, then, this does not mean there is more than one mistake. Look at the errors in relation to each other, not individually, as this is more apt to help you figure out what you did wrong. In this case the biggest clue is the start reading location. So I look there first and see the defective href. I fix the href—

> `<reference href="`**`Text/`**`ThePointBetween.xhtml#Start" title="Beginning" type="text" />`

—then redo the conversion. This time the conversion is successful.

Fig. 3.5

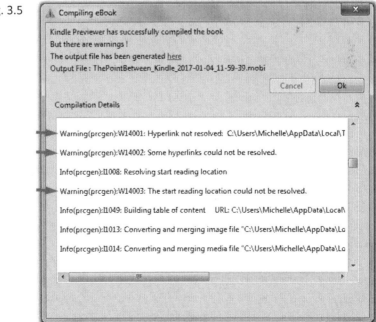

Step 9: Test Your File

In Kindle Previewer 2.94 (KP2) you can check that all your Go To menu items are working (Fig. 3.6). You can preview the file in a facsimile of a Kindle eInk device (Voyage, which is mobi8, and DX, which is mobi7), and in a Fire color device (Fire HD, Fire HDX, and HDX 8.9"). If you select Devices > Kindle for iOS, Previewer will create an AZK file; this file will not display in Previewer but can be sideloaded onto an Apple device.

By default, the mobi file will be stored in a subfolder in the same folder your Kindle ePub file is in. The subfolder name always begins with "converted" followed by your file name. The mobi file is always named the same as the converted file followed by the date and time of creation, and the file extension .mobi. You can rename as appropriate.

NOTE: Mobi files created by Kindlegen are large, usually twice the size of the ePub. This is because inside the mobi file are actually two mobi files, a mobi7 version and a mobi8 version. If you were to upload this mobi file to Amazon, their ingestion system would separate the files. If you upload this directly to a Kindle device, it does not. This duplication makes

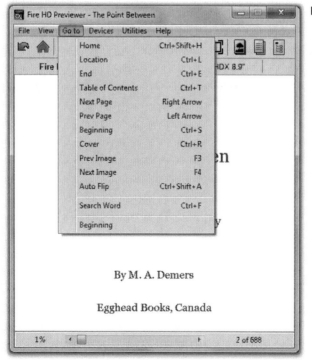

Fig. 3.6

creating your own mobi files for Advanced Review Copies, or for sending to friends, problematic if you have a large ePub to begin with.

WARNING: What you see in Kindle Previewer may not be exactly what your readers will be sent. When you upload a file to Amazon, they use a different version of Kindlegen during the ingestion process, a version withheld from the public. Amazon do not deliver mobi files to consumers; the end files are AZW (mobi7), AZW3 (mobi8), or the new KFX (mobi10).

Your file will also undergo further modifications when processed by Amazon. These include additional image processing and the aforementioned separation of the mobi7 and mobi8 files. It may also include conversion to the new KFX format.

To get an idea of the new KFX format, test in Kindle Previewer3 (KP3). The same procedure applies: download and install, then drag your ePub file over the icon, or open KP3 and drag your file into the open window.

Kindle Previewer3 previews in Fire Tablet, Kindle for Android, and Kindle e-Reader (eInk) mode. Kindle for e-Reader does not include a mobi7 option, which seems to confirm industry expectations that support for mobi7 devices will be ending soon. Selecting Kindle for iOS produces an AZK file for sideloading onto Apple devices.

Kindle Previewer3 displays the new KFX-format file, but KP3 does not produce a KFX file that you can sideload onto a device or test in your Kindle for PC or Mac app. This means you have no way of testing a KFX file except in KP3. You can export a mobi file from KP3 but the file will be the same mobi8 file that KP2 creates. To export from KP3, select the file icon in the top-left corner of the reading window, then File > Export.

One can immediately see the problem inherent in not being able to sideload a KFX file onto devices and apps for testing. At time of writing, Amazon had not expressed any plans to make such files available. Nevertheless, on the MobileRead forum a coder reported that a version of the KFX file, a KFD file, is stored in a temporary folder on your computer and can be reassembled for testing on other devices. Directions to do so are on the MobileRead thread, but lie outside the scope of this manual.

Previewer3 does not report errors as overtly as Previewer2. If your book fails conversion, a log window will open with the reason for failure. But if the file converts with errors, the log will not open automatically. Instead,

88 • Build Your Own eBooks for Free!

you have to check the conversion log by pressing Ctrl+G to see what, if anything, might be amiss.

With Previewer3 you cannot assume the file you are previewing is a KFX file. If your ebook contains formatting that is not eligible for Enhanced

Fig. 3.7

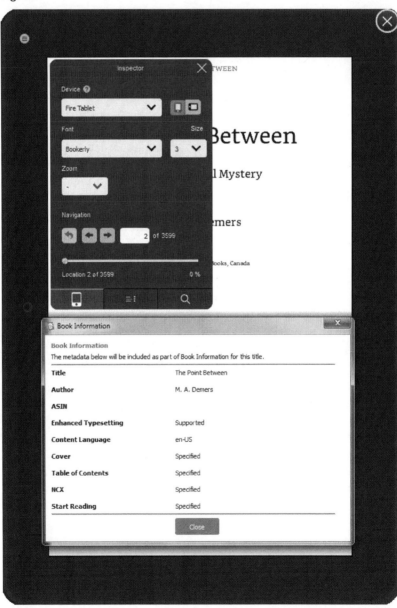

Typesetting, KP3 simply displays a mobi8 file. To check if your ebook qualifies for Enhanced Typesetting, click on File > View > Book Information (Ctrl+I). If your file qualifies, you will find "Supported" across from "Enhanced Typesetting" (Fig. 3.7).

Kindle Previewer3 also does not provide a way for you to test your Go To items. Instead, when you check your book information, a list of necessary file characteristics are listed along with whether they have been specified or not. If not, you need to find and fix the problem(s).

KFX does not support every advanced formatting option discussed next chapter, or support for an element may be limited. For example, at time of writing, tables are supported but not table captions. The reason for this limitation is that the KFX format has been, and still is being, released incrementally, with support for new features added with each release and complementary device software upgrade.

4 Advanced Formatting

As you worked through this manual and your ebook, you likely noticed patterns in the HTML code: each line of code in the body of your manuscript opens with a tag that contains the element (e.g., paragraph, heading, image), followed by the content (text, image), then usually closes with a corresponding end tag.

Elements can be further controlled by classes that determine the way in which the element is displayed, be it the style of text or the size of an image, or their positions on the screen.

Character formatting—such as Italic, Bold, and language indicators—are used to control selected text within a paragraph; character formatting uses span style tags that can, in turn, be further styled through classes.

In the CSS, elements are not prefaced with a period while styles are. This is *very* important.

The six most common elements you will find in an ebook are, as has been illustrated:

```
p   paragraph
h   heading
img image
div division
span inline styling
a   anchor (also used for href links)
```

Other common elements are:

```
hr  horizontal rule (i.e., a line)
blockquote blockquote
ul  unordered list (bullets)
ol  ordered list (numbers or letters)
table table
th  table heading
tr  table row
td  table data
caption table captions
```

We will be using these other common elements in this advanced formatting section.

The Paragraph Element

Last chapter we converted a Word document to an ebook, and so we left the Word CSS as is. However, the `p` in `p.MsoNormal` is actually redundant, and in fact limits the MsoNormal style to a paragraph style. Remove the `p` and you have a style class that can be applied to any element: a paragraph, a division, a table, and so on:

```
.MsoNormal
   {margin:0;
   margin-bottom:0;
   text-indent:3%;
   font-size:1em;}
```

Conversely, you can remove the `p.MsoNormal` class and style all body paragraphs by default:

```
p
   {margin:0;
   margin-bottom:0;
   text-indent:3%;
   font-size:1em;}
```

In the HTML you would then change all p.MsoNormal paragraphs to

```
<p>This is the first line of my chapter.</p>
```

and the paragraph would look exactly as it did originally. There is, in HTML, often more than one way to achieve the same result.

WARNING: This is a common method used by conversion companies working from a template. However, while this works in Kindle, some ePub ereaders will ignore the `<p>` formatting in the CSS and impose their own defaults if a class is not specified in the `<p>` tag. Use with caution.

Margin Attribute

While Word divides margins into their four sides, the margin attribute can be condensed into a single attribute with one to four values. It makes no difference whether you set margins as Word does or use a single line of code; however, you will often see code where the margin is a single attribute, so it is useful to know how it works.

An example of a condensed margin attribute is:

```
{margin: 0 3% 1em 5%;}
```

The values are defined starting with the top and working clockwise. In the above example, then, the top margin is 0, the right is 3%, the bottom is 1em, and the left margin is 5%.

Where any opposing margins are identical, or if all margins are the same, these can be further condensed:

```
{margin:1em 5% 1.5em;}
top margin is 1em
right and left margins are 5%
bottom margin is 1.5em

{margin:1em 5%;}
top and bottom margins are 1em
right and left margins are 5%

{margin:0;}
all four margins are 0
```

Creating New Style Classes

If you find yourself in need of a new style class, these are easy to create in your CSS. For example, you decide to add an About the Author page and want a new heading style that isn't centered like your chapter (`<h1>`) heading. To create this new style class, simply give it a new name and input the class's attributes and values. If you have an existing class that is near identical to the one you need, it is quickest to copy and paste then modify. Here I copied the `<h1>` heading and simply changed the alignment from center to left, and reduced the top margin to 0:

```
.About
  {margin-top:0em;
  margin-right:0em;
  margin-bottom:2.4em;
  margin-left:0em;
  text-align:left;
  font-size:1.8em;
  font-weight:bold;}
```

Remember that HTML elements and classes are case sensitive. If you name a class About (uppercase *A*) in your CSS but type in `<p class="about">` (lowercase *a*) in your HTML, or vice versa, the class will not be applied.

However, the order of elements and classes in your CSS, and the order of attributes within an element or class in your CSS, is irrelevant.

NOTE: The class names I use here are not mandatory; you can use whatever names you like. Just be mindful of the syntax.

New Character Classes

Character classes are created the same way as other classes, but the attributes are applied only to selected text as opposed to the paragraph it appears in; that is, character classes are always inline styling.

You can use a character class to modify font-size, font-decoration (Underline, Overline, Line-through, None), color, weight (Normal, Bold), or style (Normal, Italic). Because it is an inline style, a character class is indicated by the `<span>` tag.

Underline

If you want to underline text, you need to create a character class—

```
.underline
  {text-decoration:underline;}
```

—then apply the underline class to the text:

```
<p>The next word is <span
class="underline">underlined</span></p>
```

If an element is always underlined (a section heading, for example), you can simply add that to the element instead of applying a span class:

```
h1
  {margin-top:0em;
  margin-right:0em;
  margin-bottom:2.4em;
  margin-left:0em;
  text-align:center;
  font-size:1.8em;
  font-weight:bold;}
  font-decoration:underline;}
```

Small Caps

The Small Caps style used in Word cannot be used in an ebook, but you can fake the effect by creating a character style that decreases the font size by 10%, and then simply type in your "Small Caps" in uppercase characters:

CSS:
```
.smallcap
   {font-size:.9em;}
```

HTML:
```
<p><span class="smallcap">THIS IS THE STORY OF A MURDER.</span> Sort of.</p>
```

Drop Caps

The code below creates a drop cap that is 225% of the size of the surrounding text, or about two lines deep. Bear in mind that ereaders vary in how they wrap the text around the drop cap.

```
.drop
   {float:left;
   font-size:225%;
   line-height:1em;
   padding-right:.1em;}
```

You then code your text like this:

```
<p><span class="drop">T</span>he way to code a drop cap is like this.</p>
```

In mobi7 devices, the drop cap reverts to a larger first letter, which looks fine; there is really no need to use media queries to display the text differently in these older devices.

WARNING: Drop caps only work properly in paragraphs that are flushed left. If you use a drop cap in a paragraph with a first-line indent, the indent will start *after* the drop cap, creating a large gap between your drop cap and the rest of the word that begins your paragraph.

Multiple Classes

You can apply more than one class to an element. This avoids the need to create yet another class that combines the two.

For example, you have two classes, one for Underline and one for Small Caps—

```
.underline
   {text-decoration:underline;}

.smallcap
   {font-size:.9em;}
```

—and you want a selection of text to be both Underline and Small Caps. Rather than create a new class to do both jobs, you can apply both classes to the same span tag:

```
<p>"He went to the <span class="underline smallcap">FBI</span>!"she said with alarm.
```

Pay attention to the syntax: multiple classes are separated by a space (or semicolon if you prefer) and are contained within a single set of quotation marks.

Multiple classes can be applied to any element.

Controlling Emphasis

If used on its own, the <em> tag will produce Italic text and <strong> will produce Bold text. You can use <em> and <strong> (or <b>) together to produce emphasized Bold Italic text, for example "The sign said '***Danger! Keep Out!*** Power lines overhead.'"

However, there may be instances where you want the text to be read with emphasis but not italicized, for example when one uses All Caps to indicate a raised voice. To control the <em> tag you can create a class in your CSS. For example:

```
.noital
  {font-style:normal;}
```

Then apply the class to the <em> tag:

```
<p><em class="noital">"STOP YELLING AT ME,"</em> he yelled at me, not realizing the irony.</p>
```

As discussed in the previous section, you can apply multiple classes to any element. So if you need Small Caps and Emphasis but not Italic, you can do this:

```
<p><em class="noital smallcap">"STOP YELLING AT ME,"</em> he yelled at me, not realizing the irony.</p>
```

Adding Color

You can add color in your ebook to such things as heading text (but never body text!), to lines, frames, text boxes, and tables. However, while color will of course display on color devices, on grayscale devices these colors will display only as shades of gray.

There are 140 standard colors recognized in HTML, and are expressed either by name or by a HEX value. The official names of the supported colors and their HEX values can be found at http://www.w3schools.com/colors/colors_names.asp. For example, the official shade of the color Blue has a HEX value of #0000FF (those are zeroes, not the letter *O*). Whether you color something Blue or #0000FF in HTML, the result will be the same. If you are going to use color in your ebook, it is easiest if you restrict yourself to the official 140. For shades of gray, see http://www.w3schools.com/colors/colors_shades.asp.

WARNING: You can color headings in Word using one of its Standard colors, but Word does not strictly adhere to the official names and HEX values of the 140 HTML colors. This may require that you later change the HEX values that Word exports. This is easy enough to do in Sigil.

WARNING: On grayscale devices, and on devices in which the user can change the background color, many colors will disappear or will be rendered with insufficient contrast to be comfortably legible, particularly in Sepia Mode or Night Mode. In the *Amazon Kindle Publishing Guidelines*, Amazon provide a mathematical equation to determine legibility:

> To determine if a color falls within this range, convert your color to RGB values using a tool such as http://hex-color.com/. [Editor's note: You can also use a graphics program such as Photoshop or GIMP to do the same, and the w3schools website above also has a HEX color page.] Plug the resulting three numbers into the following formula: $Y = (0.2126 * R) + (0.7152 * G) + (0.0722 * B)$. If the value of Y falls within a range of 102 and 153, this color will create a good customer experience across Kindle devices and applications.[2]

For example, the official color Blue has a HEX value of #0000FF. This translates into R0, G0, B255. Using Amazon's formula, $Y = (0.2126 * 0) + (0.7152 * 0) + (0.0722 * 255)$; $Y = 0 + 0 + 18.411$, for a total of 18.411. This does not fall between 102 and 153. Blue is therefore not recommended by Amazon.

How you add color to the various components of your ebook is covered in each component's section.

Font Color

To add color to a font, simply add the color attribute to any relevant style. For example, to color your chapter headings red:

```
h1
   {margin-top:2.4em;
    margin-right:0;
    margin-bottom:2.4em;
    margin-left:0;
    text-align:center;
    text-indent:0;
    font-size:1.8em;
    color:red;
    font-weight:bold;}
```

or

```
h1
   {margin-top:2.4em;
    margin-right:0;
    margin-bottom:2.4em;
    margin-left:0;
    text-align:center;
    text-indent:0;
    font-size:1.8em;
    color:#FF0000;
    font-weight:bold;}
```

NOTE: Whether the color is spelled in uppercase or lowercase letters is irrelevant. Also, to avoid mindless repetition, in future examples I will only illustrate the HEX color option.

Lines

The code used by Word to create a line is not recognized by ereaders, which is why you cannot add lines to your Word document; instead, you add them in Sigil.

The lines element (`<hr>`) is recognized by ereaders. If you simply code in

```
<hr />
```

Sigil will add a 1-pixel thick, shaded white line across the whole of the screen (Fig. 4.1, default line). This will be replicated in pretty much any ereader out there.

98 • Build Your Own eBooks for Free!

NOTE: the `<hr>` element does not have a separate closing tag, which is why you need the forward slash in the opening tag.

If you want a thicker version of the shaded white line, you can add a size value into the tag. Line sizes are defined by pixels:

```
<hr size="10px" />
```

WARNING: Kindle8 devices will recognize the size attribute in the `<hr>` element, but older mobi7 devices, as well as many ePub readers, will not and will display only the default 1-pixel line. If you want anything other than the default shaded white line, you must create a CSS class that specifies the line size and apply it to the `<hr>` element.

In CSS, the border attribute controls the thickness of the line and whether it is solid, dotted, double (a solid line in a thinner box), or outset (bevelled). The default color is black. To achieve a different color, specify the value in the border attribute.

NOTE: You cannot create a shaded white line like the default one by applying the color white to the border; the line will simply disappear into

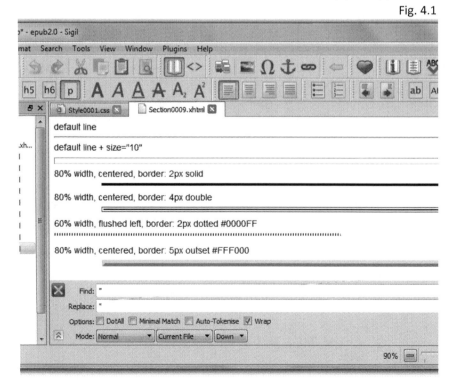

Fig. 4.1

the white screen. I have yet to learn how to create a thicker version of the default shaded white line in a way that is recognized by all ePub readers and apps.

Width defines the width of the line, which by default should be centered; however, not all devices center as they should, so to be on the safe side use the right- and left-margin attributes to control position. For example, a right- and left-margin of 10% would result in a centered line that is 80% the width of the screen. A right margin of 40% and a left margin of 0% would result in a left-aligned line that is 60% of the screen width.

The bottom margin can be set in pixels in relation to the thickness of the line, or in ems in relation to the height of the body text.

For example, hr1 is a centered, 4-pixel solid black line that is 80% of the screen width, with a bottom margin that is 2.5 times the thickness of the line:

```
.hr1
  {border:4px solid;
  margin-left:10%;
  margin-right:10%;
  margin-bottom:10px;}
```

Below, hr2 is 60% wide, left aligned, 2 pixels thick, blue, and dotted. The bottom margin is the height of a line of body text, and will increase as the user increases their ereader's display font size:

```
.hr2
  {border:2px dotted #0000FF;
  margin-right:40%;
  margin-left:0%;
  margin-bottom:1em;}
```

Once you have created your different classes, you then add whichever line(s) you want to your HTML:

```
<hr class="hr1" />
<hr class="hr2" />
```

Fig. 4.1 illustrates a few different line options. You can also combine lines by coding them without any bottom or top margins. Be as creative as you like but test in different devices and apps to ensure your lines are displaying as intended.

WARNING: Mobi7 devices cannot display anything other than a single black line, centered and 100% width; any styling will be ignored.

Blockquotes

A blockquote is a typographical term for a section of text that is set off from the main text by upper and lower margins, and inset from the left and right margins. It's another way of referring to indented blocks of text.

The blockquote element (`<blockquote>`) is another element whose values are programmed into ereaders. If you simply code part of your text in Sigil as a blockquote—

    <blockquote>Your text.</blockquote>

—Sigil will automatically inset the text (Fig. 4.2).

However, every ereader and app is programmed differently, which means you have no control over the width of the indents, which means you cannot guarantee blockquotes will align with your other paragraph indents. To overcome this, you can style the blockquote element in your CSS. For example, if you have set your body text to indent 3%, you can do the same for your blockquote:

Fig. 4.2

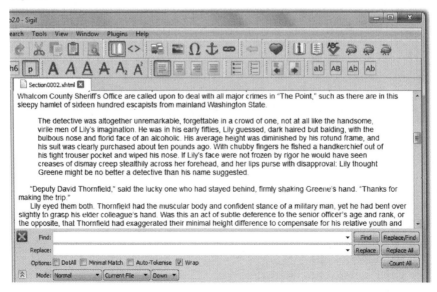

```
blockquote
  {margin-left:3%;
  margin-right:3%;}
```

If the user turns off publisher formatting, your styling will be erased but at least the blockquote will still indent as per the device's programming.

Text Boxes

A text box is simply another version of a blockquote, except that it has a border, if often modified to add a colored background, and often contains other elements such as images or lines. Text boxes are always centered on the screen, and do not allow for body text to wrap around them.

If all your text boxes are identical, and if the text does not need to be styled by a separate class in your CSS, the simplest approach is to define the blockquote element itself in your CSS. Here you can define the background color, border, and margins. Left and right margins determine the width of the box on the screen; top and bottom margins determine the distance from the preceding and following items, usually your body text.

You can also define padding, which is the space between the text and the edges of the box. Padding, like margins, is four sided (padding-top, padding-right, padding-bottom, padding-left), and you can adjust the values as you see fit.

Text can be sized (the default is 1em) and aligned (default is left).

For example, the following code creates a yellow text box with a 1-pixel solid black border around it, 10 pixels of padding between the edges of the box and its text, and is 80% the width of the screen. The text is two times (2em) the size of the surrounding body text and centered. The box is set off from the previous and next paragraphs by 1em of blank space.

NOTE: The em margins are determined by the size of the text *inside* the box, not the surrounding body text (Fig. 4.3):

```
blockquote
  {background-color:#FFFF00;
  padding:10px;
  border:1px solid;
  margin:1em 10%;
  text-size:2em;
  text-align:center;}
```

Fig. 4.3

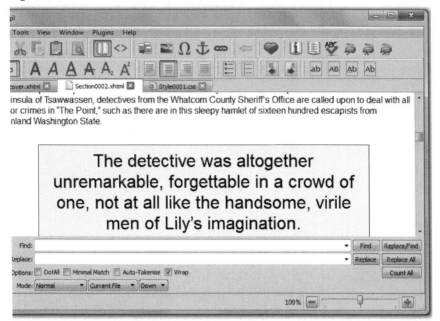

Your HTML would then look like this:

```
<blockquote>The detective was altogether
unremarkable, forgettable in a crowd of one, not
at all like the handsome, virile men of Lily's
imagination.</blockquote>
```

If, however, you need text boxes that are different from each other, you must instead create relevant classes that can be applied to divisions:

```
.box1
  {background-color:#FFFF00;
  padding:10px;
  border:1px solid;
  margin:1em 10%;
  text-size:2em;
  text-align:center;}
```

In this case, your HTML would look like this:

```
<div class="box1">The detective was altogether
unremarkable, forgettable in a crowd of one, not
at all like the handsome, virile men of Lily's
imagination.</div>
```

Text boxes can contain headings and more than one paragraph of text, and can be styled with any paragraph class found in your CSS. Text boxes can contain graphics. To do this you must bundle them all in a division, to which you apply the relevant class. In this example, the styling of the box does not include any styling of text:

```
.box2
  {background-color:#FFFF00;
  padding:10px;
  border:1px solid;
  margin:2em 10%;}
```

Text is instead styled from the existing CSS classes (Fig. 4.4):

```
<div class="box2">
  <h2>The Detective</h2>
  <hr class="hr1"/>
  <p>The detective was altogether unremarkable,
  forgettable in a crowd of one, not at all like the
  handsome, virile men of Lily's imagination…</p>
</div>
```

WARNING: The whole of the text box will disappear in mobi7 devices, leaving only the content behind. If you intend to code for both the K8 and mobi7 markets, you have two options: You can add another element to set the text off in the ebook for those reading on mobi7 devices, and set the indented text in a different font size, or perhaps bookend the text

Fig. 4.4

with a graphic or a line. In the alternative you can use media queries, explained later in this chapter. ePubs will display text boxes.

Tables and Columns

The basic table code illustrated here will work in ePubs and both K8 and mobi7 devices, though the latter will not display the content as prettily as K8 and ePub devices and apps. At time of writing, KFX displayed tables but not the caption element. This will likely have been upgraded by the time you read this manual.

With tables, you need to know a few terms:

- `border` attribute refers to the line around the table box; the value refers to the pixel width of the line. The higher the number, the thicker the line. The default style is bevelled, which becomes more noticeable the higher the value

- `width` attribute defines the percentage of the screen the table will stretch across. In the absence of this attribute, the table will size automatically according to the width of the headings or the content of the cells, whichever is greater

- `cellpadding` attribute refers to the distance from the text to the edge of the cell; the higher the value, the more white space around your data entries. In the absence of a value, the default is 0

- `cellspacing` attribute is the distance between cells; the higher the value, the greater the distance between cells. In the absence of a declared value, the default is 2. To achieve solid lines that merge, set a value of 0

- `caption` element creates a caption that sits atop the table but remains attached; it is coded *before* the table body

- `tbody` element stands for table body

- `tr` element stands for table row

- `th` element stands for table heading; a heading always

sits in a table row. By default a heading cell is bordered by a 1-pixel line

- `colspan` attribute is for headings that cross over multiple columns; the value determines the number of columns the heading cell crosses over. Colspan is used only within a table heading

- `rowspan` attribute is for headings that cross over multiple rows. Rowspan is used only within a table heading

- `td` element stands for table data; data cells always sit in a table row and by default are bordered by 1-pixel lines

By default, most ereaders will use the user-selected default font and font size, will center captions and headings, and will left align table entries.

Each `<tr>` in a table creates a table row, and each `<td>` creates a new column for that row. In each column you place your text. When you reach the end of the table row, you close it with a `</tr>`.

The following is an example of a 1-pixel border, two-column table with a caption and a single heading that crosses two columns (Fig. 4.5, top):

```
<table border="1">
  <caption>Table 1</caption>
 <tbody>
  <tr>
   <th colspan="2">Famous Self-Published Authors</th>
  </tr>

  <tr>
   <td>Women</td>
   <td>Men</td>
  </tr>

  <tr>
   <td>Virginia Woolf</td>
   <td>Mark Twain</td>
  </tr>
 </tbody>
</table>
```

In the second table I have modified the default coding by adding in cellpadding and cellspacing attributes (Fig. 4.5, bottom). The cellpadding value of 5 created more space around my cells, and therefore a larger table; the cellspacing value of 0 merged the cell borders to erase those unsightly boxes:

```
<table border="1" cellpadding="5" cellspacing="0">
```

If you do not like the default formatting, you can modify the elements in your CSS. In my next table I modified the caption to align left, I collapsed the border of the table into a single line (so no white spaces would appear between my shaded cells), and I removed the individual table data and heading cell borders so I would be left with a box only around the table:

```
caption
  {text-align:left;
  text-indent:0;}
table
  {border-collapse:collapse;}
td, th
  {border:0px;}
```

Fig. 4.5

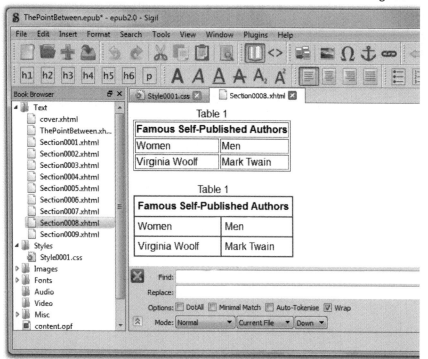

You can also create classes to control the elements. Here I created the style ttxt to control the size of the text:

```
.ttxt
  {font-size:.8em;}
```

Note also the addition of <b> to bold the column headings:

```
<td class="ttxt"><b>Women</b></td>
```

I also wanted to shade every other line in my table a light gray. To achieve this I created another class called ltgray (#E0E0E0):

```
.ltgray
  {background-color:#E0E0E0;}
```

The table was then built as below. The empty cell at the end of the "Women" column was achieved by creating a table data row but leaving it empty of text (Fig. 4.6, top).

```
<table border="1">
  <caption>Table 1</caption>

<tbody>
```

Fig. 4.6

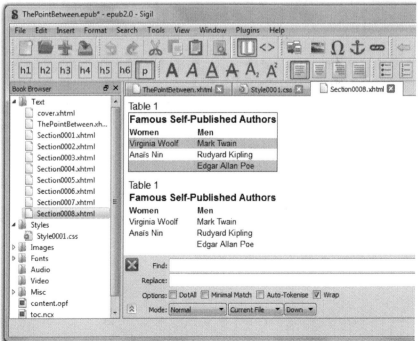

```
      <tr>
        <th colspan="2">Famous Self-Published
Authors</th>
      </tr>

      <tr>
       <td class="ttxt"><b>Women</b></td>
       <td class="ttxt"><b>Men</b></td>
      </tr>

      <tr>
       <td class="ttxt ltgray">Virginia Woolf</td>
       <td class="ttxt ltgray">Mark Twain</td>
      </tr>

      <tr>
       <td class="ttxt">Anaïs Nin</td>
       <td class="ttxt">Rudyard Kipling</td>
      </tr>

      <tr>
       <td class="ttxt ltgray"></td>
       <td class="ttxt ltgray">Edgar Allan Poe</td>
      </tr>
    </tbody>
  </table>
```

Columns are merely tables without borders; remove the border attribute from the table element (and in this case the background color in the table data cells) and you have columns instead of a table (Fig 4.6, bottom).

To create columns or tables with both top and left headings, the trick is to map it out line by line on paper first. Here I further subdivided my self-published authors by nationality and rebuilt my table as follows (Fig. 4.7):

```
    <table border="1">
      <caption>Table 1</caption>

     <tbody>
      <tr>
        <th colspan="3"><b>Famous Self-Published
Authors</b></th>
       </tr>

      <tr>
        <td></td>
         <th><b>Women</b></th>
```

Advanced Formatting • 109

```
    <th><b>Men</b></th>
 </tr>

 <tr>
  <th rowspan="2"><b>American</b></th>
    <td></td>
    <td class="ttxt">Mark Twain</td>
 </tr>

 <tr>
    <td></td>
    <td class="ttxt">Edgar Allan Poe</td>
 </tr>

 <tr>
  <th><b>British</b></th>
    <td class="ttxt">Virginia Woolf</td>
    <td class="ttxt">Rudyard Kipling</td>
 </tr>

 <tr>
  <th><b>French</b></th>
    <td class="ttxt">Anaïs Nin</td>
    <td></td>
 </tr>
 </tbody>
</table>
```

One problem you may run into is the need for different table designs that contradict each other when you define the elements in your CSS. For

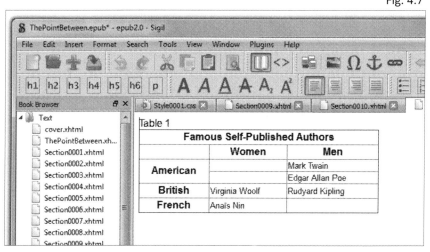

Fig. 4.7

example, you may want a border around your cells in one table but not in another. The solution is not to define the table elements in your CSS as all, but only to create classes that can be applied to each element as needed.

Increasingly complex tables can be created using other HTML tricks, but complex tables are beyond the scope of this manual. If you need to create more complex tables, you can find further help online. And always test before you assume your code will work in your ePub and Kindle formats.

Lists

Lists come in two varieties, ordered (`<ol>`) and unordered (`<ul>`). Ordered lists automatically create numbered or alphabetized lists, while unordered automatically create a bulleted list. Like blockquotes and tables, how lists are displayed is programmed individually by device manufacturers; this includes the size of the indent and the default bullet type. In ordered lists, the number or letter is always punctuated with a period. Lists are recognized in all devices.

The elements are as follows:

- `<ol>` element creates an ordered list
- `<ul>` element creates an unordered list
- `<li>` element indicates a list entry

You can specify how an ordered list is numbered:

- `style="list-style-type:arabic-numbers"` is numbered. This is the default of most ereaders and therefore does not have to be specified
- `style="list-style-type:upper-alpha"` uses uppercase letters
- `style="list-style-type:lower-alpha"` uses lowercase letters
- `style="list-style-type:upper-roman"` uses uppercase Roman numerals
- `style="list-style-type:lower-roman"` uses lowercase Roman numerals

Advanced Formatting • 111

You can specify how an ordered list is delineated:

- `style="list-style-type:disc"` for a black bullet (usually the device's default)
- `style="list-style-type:circle"` for a round white bullet with a black border
- `style="list-style-type:square"` for a black square

You can also code either ordered or unordered lists to not display a bullet of any kind:

- `style="list-style-type:none"`

A default ordered list, then, would look like this (Fig. 4.8, top):

```
<ol>
  <li>red</li>
  <li>green</li>
  <li>blue</li>
</ol>
```

A modified unordered list might look like this (Fig. 4.8, middle):

```
<ul style="list-style-type:circle">
  <li>red</li>
  <li>green</li>
  <li>blue</li>
</ul>
```

Lists can be nested, and both ordered and unordered lists can be combined (Fig. 4.8, bottom):

```
<ul>
  <li>red</li>
  <li>green
    <ol style="list-style-type:lower-alpha">
      <li>leaf green</li>
      <li>forest green</li>
    </ol>
  </li>
  <li>blue</li>
</ul>
```

As with the other standard elements, you can override the device's defaults by styling the element through your CSS. For example:

Fig. 4.8

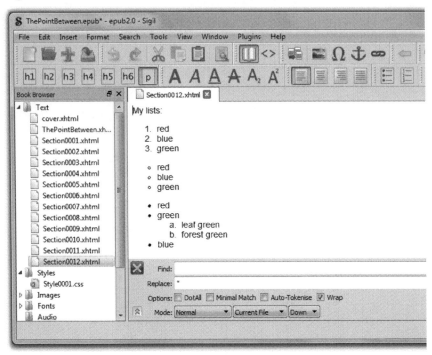

```
ol, ul
  {margin-left:3%;
  margin-bottom:1em;}
```

If not, or if publisher formatting is turned off by the user, the device's own programming will take over.

WARNING: Mobi7 devices cannot display more than one type of bullet, and ordered lists will only display in Arabic numerals.

NOTE: One problem with creating automatic lists is that you cannot use parentheses (unless you learn much more complicated code). You cannot create, for example, *1)* or *(a)* using this simplified method. If you need these you will have to create paragraph classes instead, and if so you may as well do it in Word to begin with.

Because I am usually converting to ePub from a Word document, what I do is create paragraph classes for my lists but I name these classes in such a way as to be able to find and change them easily in Sigil if I later want to convert them to HTML lists.

Editing the HTML TOC

Unlike the more restrictive NCX TOC, you can add text, sections, lines, line breaks, et cetera, to your HTML TOC. To add text, you must create the appropriate styles and add them to the sgc.toc.css; or you can link your Style0001.css to the TOC HTML file and use existing styles (an XHTML file can be linked to more than one stylesheet).

For example, in my TOC.xhtml file, just after the entry for Copyright Information—

```
<div class="sgc-toc-level-1">
   <a href="../Text/Section0001.xhtml">Copyright Information</a>
</div>
```

—I added a black line and a section title (Fig. 4.9):

```
<hr class="hr1"/>
<p class="First">Part 1: The Early Years</p>
```

This is repeated later for Part 2.

In Book View you can see the text is black instead of colored and underlined because it is not hyperlinked to anything in the ebook.

In Book View you can add line breaks anywhere just by hitting Enter as one would in a word processor. Alternatively, line breaks can be added manually in Code View by placing a break within an otherwise empty paragraph:

```
<p><br/></p>
```

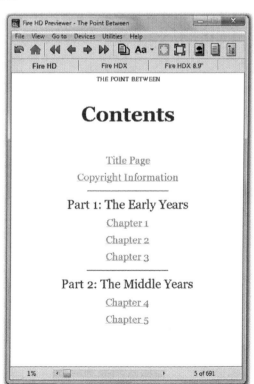

Fig. 4.9

Font Embedding

A font is actually made up of a number of separate font styles that make up a font family. Most font styles include the four basics—Regular, Bold, Italic, Bold Italic—and can also include styles such as Black, Light, Semibold, Slanted, Condensed, Medium, Narrow, and Demibold. When you use Times New Roman (TNR) as your font and you italicize selected text, the TNR Regular font is replaced by its sibling TNR Italic; if you bold the text, it is replaced by TNR Bold; and if you bold and italicize the text, it is replaced by TNR Bold Italic.

When you export your book to a PDF for print, your font is not exported as a single font family but as its separate font styles, and is embedded in the PDF. When you export your text to HTML for an ebook, however, the font-family definition (i.e., the name of the font) is exported but not the font itself. Instead, fonts found in an ereader have been licensed by the device manufacturer, and usually these fonts each contain the four basic font styles. If not, the device will fake the missing style, using an algorithm to slant the text for Italic, or to thicken the text for Bold.

As noted in the earlier chapter, ebooks are designed to allow the user to choose which font they wish to read your book in. However, there are times when that is not practical or desired. For example, to illustrate the code in this book I purposely coded in the Monospace font. Another example is an author who embeds a handwriting font to mimic handwritten letters that form part of the narrative.

Embedded fonts can be either TTF (True Type Font) or OTF (Open Type Font), though OTF is preferred. Type-1 (Postscript) fonts are not allowed.

Font Licensing Versus Open Source

Fonts are copyrighted and owned either by individual designers or by font foundries, the companies who own the fonts you are using on your computer. When ebooks became popular, font foundries declared that font embedding in ebooks is copyright infringement and demanded that publishers pay a licence fee to use. Most fees are exorbitant and well beyond the means of the average self-publisher. This means that authors who need to embed a font in their ebook but do not want to pay a licence fee have to find open-source fonts on the Internet. The number of open-source fonts available has increased over the last two years, including from the likes of Adobe, but they are still few in number and many do not contain the four font styles you may require. Not all allow embedding; although the font is declared open source, you will still need to read the End User Licence Agreement (EULA) to make sure it allows embedding in ebooks.

If you use a licensed font, the EULA will also likely insist that you obfuscate the font to prevent a user from lifting the font from your ePub. You can do this in Sigil.

Fonts are also large files and thus they will cause your ebook file to increase in size, which makes your ebook more expensive to deliver on Amazon because Kindle Direct Publishing charges the publisher a delivery fee per megabyte. There is a way to decrease the font size if you are only using a few characters, which I will illustrate shortly.

Monospace Font

Kindle readers and apps, and many ePub devices and apps, have a hidden font, a Courier-like font called Monospace. If you define the font-family as Monospace, this font will display without the need to embed it. Monospace is used in this ebook to replicate HTML:

```
p.Code
   {margin-top:0;
   margin-bottom:0;
   margin-left:5%;
   text-indent:0%;
   text-align:left;
   font-size:1em;
   font-family:monospace;}
```

WARNING: While Kindles do not care if the font name is capitalized or lowercase, the ePub devices and apps that I tested only displayed correctly when the font was spelled in lowercase.

WARNING: Monospace is by no means universal among ePub devices and apps. If the font is integral to your ebook, embed it.

Unicode

You may recall that the encoding in your ebook is UTF-8, which stands for Unicode Transformation Format 8. Unicode is now the computer industry's standard method of encoding text and symbols that make up all the languages of the world and the many common symbols such as those found in the fonts Webdings and Wingdings. Unfortunately, the vast number of Unicode characters and symbols (there are currently 128,000) is both its blessing and its curse.

The problem is that ebook devices and apps vary greatly in the number of Unicode characters that are programmed into the ereader, and may also vary within the fonts licensed by the device or app manufacturer. When I tested ten random Unicode characters in an ebook, Kindle displayed five of the ten, my Kobo Touch displayed four, and Adobe Digital Editions only displayed three. Sigil itself is also limited in how many Unicode characters it can display. Characters that do not display are replaced with either blank spaces or an empty white box with either an *X* or a *?* in it.

To use a Unicode character you need to know its equivalent HTML HEX numeric code. To figure *that* out, you first need to know the Unicode character code. The official site for this is http://unicode.org/charts/; the webpage is then subdivided into languages and into symbols and punctuation. You can also google "Unicode characters" and check other pages such as Wikipedia.

WARNING: The symbols are not always easy to find. For example, some musical symbols are found under Miscellaneous Symbols instead of under Musical Symbols. This is because the Unicode system is continually evolving; many of the early, now common symbols were lumped together under Miscellaneous in the early days of development.

The formula to convert Unicode to HTML HEX is:

&#x + (the Unicode character code - U+) + ;

For example, for the musical cleft symbol the Unicode character code is U+1d120. Its HTML HEX code is therefore "𝄠". In Sigil, if while in Code View you type in `&#x1d120;` as if it were a word in a sentence in your ebook, when you switch to Book View you will see the cleft symbol appear. For many common symbols, Sigil will replace the Unicode formula in Code View with the corresponding symbol when you save your document.

The only way to know if your Unicode characters and symbols will display is to put them in and test. If you need a Unicode character or symbol that does not display, you can embed a Unicode font. There are open-source Unicode fonts available that are free to embed in ebooks, but all vary in the number of characters and symbols included; make sure the one you choose meets your needs. Search online and always check the End User Licence Agreement (EULA).

How to Embed a Font

In Sigil, right-click on the Fonts folder and select Add Existing Files... Navigate to the font in your computer and select it.

Once the font is embedded in the ebook, you need to tell the CSS that the font is there and where to find it. In this example I have embedded the Adobe open-source font SourceSansPro in all four styles. I therefore opened my Style0001.css and at the top I added the following code for each font style embedded. **Pay attention to the font weights and styles for the different font faces:**

```
@font-face
  {font-family:"SourceSansPro-Regular";
  font-weight:normal;
  font-style:normal;
  src:url("../Fonts/SourceSansPro-Regular.otf");}

@font-face
  {font-family:"SourceSansPro-It";
  font-weight:normal;
  font-style:italic;
  src:url("../Fonts/SourceSansPro-It.otf");}

@font-face
  {font-family:"SourceSansPro-Bold";
  font-weight:bold;
  font-style:normal;
  src:url("../Fonts/SourceSansPro-Bold.otf");}

@font-face
  {font-family:"SourceSansPro-BoldIt";
  font-weight:bold;
  font-style:italic;
  src: url("../Fonts/SourceSansPro-BoldIt.otf");}
```

Wherever you want this font to appear, you add it to the relevant CSS styles. For example:

```
.Letter
  {font-size:1em;
  font-family:SourceSansPro-Regular;}
```

When using a device's font, the formatting tags `<em>`, `<strong>`, `<i>`, and `<b>` work because the device has the Italic and Bold font styles installed and is programmed to use them. However, when you embed a font you cannot simply apply formatting tags to your text; you also need to tell the ereader to apply the appropriate font family. To do this, create a CSS class for every font face except Regular:

```
.SSPi
  {font-family:"SourceSansPro-It";
  font-weight:normal;
  font-style:italic;}
.SSPb
  {font-family:"SourceSansPro-Bold";
  font-weight:bold;
  font-style:normal;}
.SSPbi
  {font-family:"SourceSansPro-BoldIt";
  font-weight:bold;
  font-style:italic;}
```

In your HTML you would then add the class to the tag:

```
<p class="Letter">My <em class="SSPi">darling</em> Jane</p>
```

WARNING: If you use an embedded font in your ebook, it is recommended that you place a warning at the front of your book indicating this and advising readers not to turn off publisher formatting.

NOTE: If you embed a font in your ePub, when you convert into the mobi file in Kindle Previewer2 you will get a warning that a font has been embedded and that it may not display as intended across all devices. This is because mobi7 devices cannot display embedded fonts. Also, some publishers have reported issues with Amazon deleting font-family attributes despite font embedding. Check your file with Amazon before sale.

NOTE: If you embed a font and use the W3C validation tool, it will return errors regarding the fonts attributes and values. Ignore this as it does not refer to ebooks. When you validate your ePub, the code will pass.

Font Obfuscation

If using a licensed font that requires obfuscation, right-click on the font. In the menu will be the option for Font Obfuscation and another submenu with the options None (checked by default), Use Adobe's Method, and

Use IDPF's Method. Without my going into the convoluted reasons why, choose Use IDPF's Method; it's the lesser of the two evils.

Apple Plugin

Apple once again rears their annoying head here. While ePubs and Kindle books are content with the above code, Apple insists on another bit of code (that absolutely no one else uses) in order for Apple's iBooks reader to recognize an embedded font. If you intend to sell through Apple, you will need to download the **Sigil plugin AddiBooksXML**.

Sigil plugins are created by the group of coders who make up Sigil's voluntary development team. Currently, a list of available plugins is on the MobileRead forum at http://www.mobileread.com/forums/showthread.php?t=247431. AddiBooksXML is currently at http://www.mobileread.com/forums/showthread.php?t=272241. If by the time you read this these threads have moved, simply check the main Sigil section on MobileRead; a sticky post for plugins is found there.

Download to your computer and unzip the zip file at the bottom of the post by DiapDealer. In Sigil, from the toolbar select Plugins > Manage

Fig. 4.10

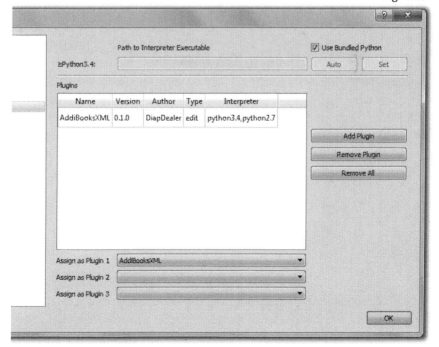

Plugins. In the window that opens, click on Add Plugin. Navigate to the folder where you stored the plugin zip file. Select the *zip file* and click on Open. The plugin will now be added to Sigil (Fig. 4.10).

Although optional, at the bottom of the window you can assign the plugin to a toolbar icon to create a shortcut.

To add the code, from the toolbar select Plugins > Edit > AddiBooksXML. When it executes it will open a navigation window. Navigate to the folder where you unzipped the archive and select the plugin.xml file.

In your Book Browser, in the Misc folder, will now appear a file named com.apple.ibooks.display-options.xml.

This additional file does not affect your ePub's performance in other ereaders or apps, so you can use the same file to distribute to both Apple and other retailers.

WARNING: Once you have this file created in your ebook, you cannot simply export the file to your computer from Sigil and use it again in a future ebook by copying it into the Misc folder. Although this XML file appears in the Misc folder in your Book Browser, the file actually resides in the ebook's META-INF file, which would otherwise have to be manually edited and your ebook rebuilt.

Subset Your Font(s) (optional)

Fonts are large files and will therefore add to the cost of delivering your ebook on Amazon. If you also have a lot of images in your ebook, the addition of large fonts may put your ebook in excess of file-size limits imposed by retailers.

One way around this is to subset the font. This is particularly useful if you are only using a few characters. Subsetting takes a bit of work, and another open-source program to achieve, but it's easy enough to do and can shave a great deal of the font size off your ePub.

To subset the font, first download and install the ebook management program **Calibre** (https://calibre-ebook.com/download).

Open Calibre. From the toolbar, select "Add books". Navigate to your finished ePub and click Open. Calibre will add the ePub to your Calibre library (Fig. 4.11).

Advanced Formatting • 121

Fig. 4.11 (top) and Fig. 4.12 (bottom)

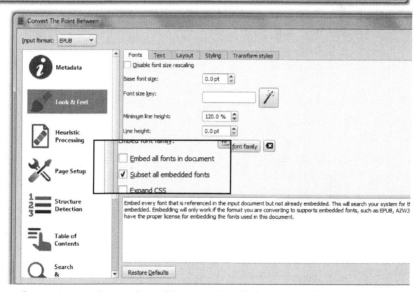

Now from the toolbar select "Convert books". In the dialogue box that opens, in the "Output format" field (in the upper-right corner) select "EPUB".

In the left window frame, select Look & Feel. Under the Fonts tab, check "Subset all embedded fonts". Click OK (Fig. 4.12). Calibre will now make a new ePub with a subsetted font.

Open this new ePub in Sigil. (Don't worry that your ebook is now likely messed up; you will not be using this file.) Under the Fonts folder, click on the font and select Save As… Save the font to your computer.

Now return to your original ePub. Delete the original, larger font and replace it with the smaller subset font Calibre created for you.

Internal Images

The first issue you must deal with in regard to internal images is that of image size, specifically the issue of having to keep pace with the development of large-screen, high-resolution devices.

Early ebook screens were, on average, no more than around 600 x 1024 pixels; that meant an image of 1000 pixels on the long side would be sufficient to fill the screen. But now the major manufacturers are producing eInk devices with screens that are approximately 1440 pixels (Kindle Oasis, Nook Glowlight) to 1872 pixels (Kobo Aura One) on the long side. Color tablets targeted at ebook readers are as tall as 2048 pixels (Samsung Galaxy Tab S2 for Nook). In such devices, those older 1000-pixel images only fill 50–70% of the screen.

If the image is smaller than the screen and is coded to display at larger than its native pixel dimensions, in most devices the image is upsized. This causes artifacts, which are noticeable off-color pixels in areas of high contrast that create a telltale ghosting effect. Upsized images are also subjected by the device to an anti-aliasing filter, which removes the hard pixelation that upsizing causes but does so by blurring the edges between pixels. This blurring causes obvious image softening. Between the artifacts and anti-aliasing, images become obviously degraded. If your images contain text, the text can become illegible or at the very least harder to read.

Image upsizing is particularly an issue on the iPad because of its Retina screen. Retina screens compress pixels, which then requires more pixels to achieve the same display size as other screens. Essentially, take the problem of upsizing and anti-aliasing on other devices and multiply it by 1.5 to 2 times. And some more again for the 12.9" iPad Pro, which is 2732 pixels tall.

The issues created by larger screens is exacerbated by higher resolutions. In 2012, when I first began writing for self-published authors, the highest resolution color screen was the iPad at 132 ppi (pixels per inch); today, the iPad3 is 264 ppi and you can find smartphones with screen resolutions of over 400 ppi. Grayscale devices have increased from an average 170 ppi to 300 ppi in the most common models, namely Kindle, Kobo, and Nook.

The higher the resolution of the device screen, the smaller the image displays at its native size. For example, if an image is 900 pixels high, on an old 170-ppi screen that image would display at a little over 5.25" high (900 pixels / 170 pixels per inch = 5.294"). On a 300-ppi screen, that same image now only displays at 3" high.

The larger and higher resolution the viewing device, the greater the number of image pixels required to achieve a crisp and legible image. The more pixels, the larger the image file; the larger the image file, the larger the ebook file. The larger the ebook file the longer it takes to download to the consumer's device and the more memory it takes to store. As a consequence, all the major retailers place file size limits both on individual images and ebooks as a whole even as these same retailers keep making larger screens that demand larger image files. And Amazon add injury to insult by charging publishers a delivery fee based on the file size, a direct hit on our profits. It's a no-win situation for us.

The third issue you will need to tackle is image coding. This is where building ePubs becomes infernally frustrating. While Amazon's closed ecosystem has resulted in a single, easy method to ensure images work on all Kindle devices and apps, ePub device manufacturers and app developers have been all over the map.

I believe the problem arose from the desire of device and app manufacturers to coerce consumers into retailer loyalty. Amazon for the most part achieve consumer loyalty by selling a different, proprietary format, but ePub retailers have had to resort to different methods. Originally, loyalty was coerced through Digital Rights Management (DRM), but the more DRM came under fire, and the more people resorted to cracking it, the more manufacturers began using device and app programming as a way to achieve the same objective. Image display was the first casualty; we have already seen this with the issue of Apple and ebook covers. Now you will see it in operation with internal images.

Image Size and Format

Kindle

Amazon allow JPEG, GIF, BMP, PNG, and SVG formats, to a maximum of 5MB, saved at 300 ppi, in sRGB or grayscale. No transparency is allowed. Save at the highest quality you can while remaining within the file size limit.

Amazon Kindle Publishing Guidelines recommends that images display clearly at 2X the intended magnification to accommodate Amazon's HDX screens. However, I believe this is merely Amazon-speak for accommodating users reading Kindle books on Apple Retina devices. And in any case Amazon have abandoned their HDX line of tablets; the latest Fire HD tablets are only 1280 pixels high.

With that in mind, I would recommend aiming for around 1800 pixels on the long side, which is the height of the latest dedicated Kindle eInk device, the Oasis. If you want to accommodate the previous Kindle HDX tablet market, aim for 2500 pixels on the long side. You can accommodate the iOS market with even larger images, but bear in mind this will increase your file size significantly.

Your large images are then processed by Amazon into various sizes for different devices: larger-screen, higher-resolution devices are sent larger image files while smaller, lower-resolution devices are sent smaller image files. Publishers are charged a delivery fee based on the smallest file produced for older Kindle devices, not the larger files sent to, for example, an iPad. That said, as Amazon phases out these older mobi7 devices, publishers can expect the cost of delivery to increase.

Photographs must be JPEGs, and 600 x 800 pixels at minimum, but such small images are of little use. Such a photograph would, at its native size, display at only 2.7" high on a 300-ppi screen (800 pixels / 300 pixels per inch = 2.7"). Small images suffer from the image degradation discussed in the previous section.

For charts and tables presented as images, and for simple graphics such as logos, Amazon want these embedded as GIFs. If the graphic contains text, the lower case *a* must be no less than 6 pixels high.

Amazon accept SVG images but there are strict rules. Consult *Amazon Kindle Publishing Guidelines* if you intend to use SVG images.

Kobo

Kobo readers can display images of any size but no greater than 5MB is recommended for optimal display across platforms; Kobo advise that images over 3MB will not improve display. Kobo readers will display GIF, JPEG, and PNGs; Kobo offer limited support for SVG. Images should be in sRGB or grayscale, 300 ppi, and saved at the highest quality within the file size limit. No transparency is allowed.

Apple

Images should be submitted as large as possible to a maximum of 4M pixels, saved at 300 ppi. Captions must not be embedded in images. Images must be JPEGs or PNGs, in sRGB or grayscale. If there are areas of transparency, use PNG or JPEGs with WebKit PNG masks.

Apple state that no text can be presented as images as this prevents the user from searching the text. This suggests that tables and other similar graphics can only be presented in HTML.

To accommodate the Retina screen, images should contain at least 1.5 times the size of the target display size; that is, if you want an image to display at 1000 pixels wide, you need to embed an image that is 1500 to 2000 pixels wide. This further complicates matters with Apple: with the exception of the 12.9" iPad Pro at 2732 x 2048 pixels, all other current iPads have screens of 2048 x 1536 pixels, for a total of 3,145,728 pixels. While this is within the limit of 4M pixels, multiply by 1.5 and now you have 4.7M pixels, which will cause Apple to reject your ebook.

Tap and Zoom Function

Most tablet ereader devices, and many newer-model eInk devices, allow the user to tap on an image to see it displayed "outside" the text. In some devices the tapped image is sized to fill the screen; in other devices the image is displayed at its native pixel dimensions if smaller than the screen. If the image is small, this can result in the tapped image displaying smaller (but sharper) than when "inside" the text.

XHTML File Size Limit

Both Apple and Kobo state that individual XHTML files in an ebook cannot exceed 10MB. If you have many images in an XHTML file, you will need to split it further in Sigil. Note that the order of the XHTML files in your ebook, not the name or number of the files, determines the order of display.

For example, if after initially splitting your file you have ten XHTML files, and you then split Section0005.xhtml after putting images in it, Sigil will create Section0011.xhtml and place it after Section005.xhtml. This is perfectly fine and will in no way mess up your ebook.

Standard HTML Coding

The standard coding used by most ebook designers is simple: in the `<img>` tag add a height (for vertical images) or width (for horizontal images) attribute with a value of 100%:

```
<img alt="MyImage" height="100%" src="../Images/
MyImage.jpg"/>
```

or

```
<img alt="MyImage" width="100%" src="../Images/
MyImage.jpg"/>
```

The height or width value causes the image to display at 100% of the height or width of the screen (less the book margins), and prevents a large image from failing to downsize to fit a smaller screen.

WARNING: If you do not put in a size value, and the pixel dimensions of your image are larger than the screen, in many ereaders your image will not be downsized to fit; it will be cropped.

To display an image at less than 100% of the screen, simply adjust the height or width value.

To center or right align an image, you must place the image in a division and align the division:

```
<div style="text-align:center">
<img alt="MyImage" width="50%" src="../Images/
MyImage.jpg"/>
</div>
```

The advantage of this method is that it is not CSS dependent; if the user turns off publisher formatting, your images will still be scaled and positioned as coded.

Adding Captions

A caption can be made using any style class, and is contained within the division:

```
<div style="text-align:center">
<img alt="MyImage" height="50%" src="../Images/
MyImage.jpg"/>
<p class="cap">My image caption.</p>
</div>
```

Note that you cannot use the `<caption>` element because it is restricted to tables.

To keep the caption from separating from the image, you can add a page-break-inside attribute with the value "avoid":

```
<div style="text-align: center; page-break-
inside:avoid">
```

Pay attention to the syntax when applying more than one style attribute to a division: style attributes and their values are separated from each other by a semicolon and surrounded by a single set of quotation marks.

WARNING: The page-break-inside attribute is not recognized by Kindle devices. If the image fits on the page but the caption does not, the caption will be pushed to the next screen. It is for this reason that Amazon direct publishers to place image captions only below images.

With ePub readers that recognize the attribute, the image and caption will remain attached and will, if necessary, be pushed together to the next screen. However, this is dependent on the combined image and caption equalling less than 100% of the screen.

It is important to recognize, then, that **an image cannot be 100% of the screen height *and* contain an attached caption.** Often the image cannot be more than 85–90% of the screen height, less if the caption is lengthy. If the caption is too long to fit, it will be pushed to the next screen regardless of the page-break-inside attribute.

The same issue will apply to horizontal images if the user rotates their screen. There isn't much you can do about this as it will all depend on the image height relative to the screen height when in horizontal mode.

Apple

As you may have gathered by now, Apple's method of image handling is to wrap images in divisions; the division keeps the image from splitting over screens. As with the cover, Apple devices are designed not to read image size in the image tag.

Some publishers claim that Apple devices do read height and/or width attributes in the image tag, just that Apple do not admit this. Not having tested every Apple device, I can neither confirm nor deny this. What

I can tell you for certain is that Apple's own technical papers say that this information in the image tag is not read. What I can also confirm is that Apple devices regularly split images over two screens if the image is not placed in a division and the image displays partway down the screen. A workaround some publishers may be using is to always place the image in its own XHTML file, or to add a page break before every image; both options force such images to the top of the next screen, even if that leaves text orphaned on the preceding screen. Images do not then split over two screens because they always have a full screen to work with.

In the preceding chapter, I replicated the CSS code Apple want for images:

```
img
   {height:100%;}
.image-container
   {height:100%;
   text-align:center;}
```

And in your HTML:

```
<div class="image-container">
<img alt="MyImage" src="../Images/MyImage.jpg"/>
</div>
```

whereby the JPEG title is the name of your image file.

While this works fine if you only have vertical images designed to fill the screen, you run into problems if you have horizontal images, or you have vertical images you wish to display at less than 100% height (with an attached caption, for example).

If so, you have to delete from your CSS

```
img
   {height:100%;}
.image-container
   {height:100%;
   text-align:center;}
```

and instead create two classes, one vertical, one horizontal, that can be applied to the image tag as needed:

```
.ver
   {height:100%;}
.hor
   {width:100%;}
```

And you need to create at least two image containers, one for vertical images and one for horizontal images:

```
.V100
   {height:100%;}
.H100
   {width:100%;}
```

In your HTML, you would then have this for example:

```
<div class="V100">
<img class="ver" alt="MyImage" src="../Images/MyImage.jpg"/>
</div>
```

(I like to use the format of *V* for *vertical* and *H* for *horizontal*, followed by the percentage, as I later then do not have to try to remember my class names as I work through my images.)

By default, images are left aligned. If you want your images to be centered or right aligned on the screen, you can add a text-align attribute to the container class or create a separate class whose sole function is to position the content, in this case center it—

```
.center
 {text-align:center;}
```

—and apply it as needed to the division:

```
<div class="V100 center">
```

If you have images that are not intended to fill the screen, you have to create an image container for every size you want. In case you decide to use a caption, you can add the page-break-inside attribute too. For example:

```
.V85
   {height:85%;
   page-break-inside:avoid;}
```

This would create an image container that is 85% of the screen height. With horizontal images that are less than 100% of the screen, using the text-align attribute to center images usually does not work. If so, use the left- and right-margin attributes to achieve the same effect. For example, if you need an image to be 85% of the screen width and centered, use something like this:

```
.H85
  {margin-left:7.5%;
  margin-right:7.5%;
  page-break-inside:avoid;}
```

The problem with the Apple method of using divisions is that it is dependent on the user *not* turning off publisher formatting, which, as noted before, will break the link to the CSS. This method is also far more time-consuming and convoluted. This is why most ebook designers loathe this method and will not do it unless paid extra to produce an Apple-specific file.

However, Apple devices are popular, and major retailers such as Amazon, Kobo, and Google Play want to sell to this large consumer base. These retailers have produced iOS apps, but there are many Apple users who prefer to purchase ePubs and read on the default Apple iBooks reader (the one whose programming necessitates containers). I believe it is for this reason that both Kobo and Google Play now request the CSS method be used for image sizing. Which method you choose is dependent on where you want to sell and whether or not you are willing to do the work to accommodate Apple iBooks users.

Combined Method

Last chapter I suggested adding backup HTML as a way to ensure your images display correctly if the user disables publisher formatting. This can be done here too. For example, your horizontal image is 50% of the screen width and centered. You have a caption below it. You have built the necessary classes. Now you add the backup HTML:

```
<div class="h50 center" style="text-align: center;
page-break-inside:avoid">
<img class="hor" alt="My Image" src="../Images/
MyImage.jpg" width="50%"/>
<p class="cap">Caption</p>
</div>
```

You can add the text-align code manually or by using the Center icon in Sigil.

Inline Images

An inline image is one that does not sit apart from the text but forms part of the sentence. An example would be a translation of Chinese characters into English:

> The Chinese character for Qi is 氣.

Such images cannot be placed in frames. Instead, the image is placed within the paragraph itself and the height is kept in line with the text by setting the height as an em value in the CSS:

```
CSS:
.1em
  {height:1em;}

HTML:
<p>The Chinese character for Qi is <img
class="1em" alt="Ki" src="../Images/Ki.jpg"/>.</p>
```

Inline images are finicky and some ereaders do not display them correctly (or not at all), ignoring the class and instead displaying the image at its native dimensions and completely skewing the text; it's definitely hit and miss.

Since so many foreign-language characters, Webdings, and Wingdings are now found in the Unicode font, inline images have become essentially obsolete (except for mobi7 devices, which cannot read embedded fonts). It is certainly preferable to use Unicode as this avoids most size and display issues. Again, though, remind your readers that you have an embedded font, and that turning off publisher formatting will erase this.

If you want to accommodate mobi7 users, I recommend you use inline images and media queries for the mobi7 format only, and keep the images really small so they display at least somewhat correctly. Know, though, that you cannot rely on this.

Frames

A frame is a box that can be "floated" left or right, and which allows text to flow around it; frames are the ebook equivalent of sidebars. Because frames can contain images, they are a way to create left- or right-aligned images with text wrap. (Frames cannot be centered with text flowing down both sides.)

Frames are set as a percentage of the container (i.e., the screen) size, and images within frames are set as a percentage of the frame. So if you want your image to be 50% of the screen width, then you would create a frame that is 50% wide and set the image size to 100%.

You set your border width, style, and color in the frame class, and if you want some space between the content and the frame you use the padding attribute. If you want some space between the frame and surrounding text, you use the margin attribute. For example:

```
.FrameLeft
  {border:1px solid;
  padding:5px;
  float:left;
  width:50%;
  margin: 10px 10px 10px 0px;}
```

In your document, you then place the contents of your frame in a division to which you apply the frame class. Fig. 4.13 was achieved with the following HTML (with the text reduced for our purposes here):

```
<h1>There's more to good and evil than meets the eye…</h1>

<div class="FrameLeft">
   <img alt="Baby_Jane450" src="../Images/Baby_Jane450.jpg" width="100%"/>
   <p class="cap"><i>Baby Jane</i> by M.A. Demers.</p>
</div>

<p class="First">When human remains are found in her pre-war fixer-upper in an east Vancouver neighbourhood,</p>
```

NOTE: The text you want to wrap alongside the image is placed *after* the frame.

WARNING: If you coded your cover or internal images to accommodate Apple, the above image frame will not work because of the `img {height:100%;}` element in your CSS you were forced to put in.

If you coded for Apple, here you instead have to add the `hor` class to the `<img>` **tag:**

```
<div class="FrameLeft">
  <img class="hor" alt="Baby_Jane450" src="../
Images/Baby_Jane450.jpg" width="100%"/>
  <p class="cap"><i>Baby Jane</i> by M.A.
Demers.</p>
</div>
```

WARNING: Many ereaders are unreliable in keeping the frame and surrounding text aligned as coded, especially if the user increases the font size on their screen. Use with caution and always test in different devices if possible and in different user font sizes.

WARNING: Frames do not display in mobi7 devices. Use media queries for mobi7 users if this is an issue for you.

Fig. 4.13

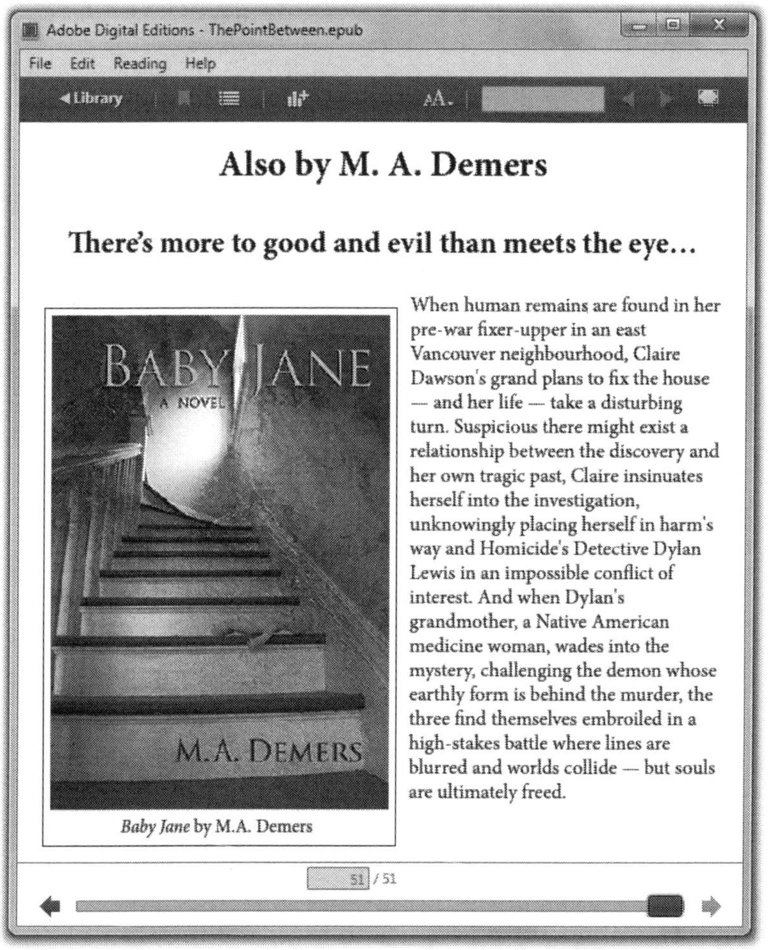

Kindle Media Queries

As you have seen in this manual, Amazon's older mobi7 devices are quite rudimentary: all your K8 styling disappears along with your hard work. As a publisher you have two choices, ignore this part of the market or use media queries to create alternate display options for mobi7 customers.

Many publishers now choose to ignore the mobi7 market. Why? Because it is a very small (and continually shrinking) part of the market and the time or money spent to create additional mobi7 code is deemed unfeasible. Moreover, if you are creating ebooks more complex than a novel, it is likely that your target audience is using a K8 device or an updated Kindle app on a tablet or laptop.

Often K8 styling is merely erased in mobi7 devices but the content remains. In many cases this in itself does not cause issues. Where you do run into problems is with things like inline images, cascading indents, text boxes, frames, and tables.

If you want to accommodate this tiny market, you first need to create alternate content and classes, if necessary, for your mobi7 consumers. This might include using an image of your table instead of displaying the HTML table, or using a different-sized font between lines that mimic the top and bottom borders of a text box. Cascading indents can be created using nested blockquotes.

Once you have decided how to present your K8 content to a mobi7 audience, you use media queries to define which content is displayed based on the device used. A media query merely asks the device "What are you?" then displays the appropriate version of content while hiding the alternative.

To create media queries, first add the following code to your Kindle book's CSS:

```
.defaultcontent
    {display:block;}
.mobicontent
    {display:none;}
@media amzn-mobi {
    .defaultcontent
    {display:none;}
    .mobicontent
    {display:block;}
}
```

Then, in your HTML, wherever you have alternative content, you define each as either default or mobi. For example, here a K8 (`"default"`) text box is replaced by two lines and indented, smaller text for the mobi7 (`"mobi"`) version:

```
<div class="default">
 <div class="box1">
  <h2>The Detective</h2>
  <hr class="hr1"/>
  <p>Your text here.</p>
 </div>
</div>

<div class="mobi">
   <hr/>
   <h2>The Detective</h2>
   <blockquote class="ttxt">Your text here.</blockquote>
   <hr/>
</div>
```

Endnotes

1. If you do hire out your ebook design, it is important that you ask for the *ePub source file for your Kindle book and not the mobi file*: you cannot edit a mobi file but you can edit the source ePub in Sigil. If your designer will not provide you with the source ePub, shop around for another ebook designer.

2. Amazon Inc., *Amazon Kindle Publishing Guidelines: How to make books available for the Kindle platform, Version 2017.1*, 25.

About M. A. Demers

M. A. Demers is a writer, editor and self-publishing consultant with a diverse clientele as far away as Australia and Columbia. In 2011 she self-published her first novel, *Baby Jane*, followed by *The Global Indie Author: Your Guide to the World of Self-Publishing*, now in its third edition, and the concise *To Kindle in Ten Steps: The Easy Way to Format, Create and Self-Publish an eBook on Amazon's Kindle Direct Publishing*. In 2015 she published her second novel, *The Point Between*.

Made in the USA
Columbia, SC
05 May 2017